Prai

The Visible Lawyer
and Douglas McPherson

'Bringing together practical tips, common sense, modern marketing theory, and a deep understanding of the challenges, motivations, and difficulties faced by all professionals, this book is a must read for all lawyers wanting to maximise their business development and marketing impact in tough, competitive times.'

Lance Sapsford, director of business development and marketing, London at Ince & Co

'Doug really knows his stuff. He has demystified business development (or whatever you want to call it) and has focused on getting and retaining clients through the neat concept of simply being "visible". This book contains useful insights and practical help to guide the busy lawyer through an area that does not always come naturally to many of them, but is of vital importance to their and their firm's future prosperity.'

John Seigal, managing partner at Clintons Solicitors

'Lawyers love a check list – and *The Visible Lawyer* provides a very accessible, practical, and usable tool for any lawyer looking for a straightforward, no-nonsense guide on how to do this "BD thing". Don't waste time worrying about doing BD or shaking in the corner at a networking event; get this book, use it to draw up your own plan that works for you, let your confidence and effectiveness grow, and reap the rewards.'

Neil Cormack, head of marketing and business development at Lupton Fawcett

'If you're looking for a guide as to how to improve (or even start) as an entrepreneurial, business-generating lawyer then look no further. Doug McPherson has put together a book which is long on practical tips and examples and, thankfully, short on marketing speak. It makes a rewarding read.'
David Williams, chairman of Geldards LLP

'When it comes to working with BD consultants, Doug is breath of fresh air. His ability to listen and get to the heart of an issue quickly enables him to deliver focused strategic thinking that will take your business forward.

Having previously worked in several ad agencies, I can safely say that Doug is the best copywriter I've ever worked with! Backed with his understanding of your strategic direction and the marketplace, Doug's easy yet concise copy style will give you the tools to communicate your proposition clearly to your target audience using plain English.

I would recommend Doug to anyone looking for a business partner to challenge the status quo within the professional services environment – you won't be disappointed.'
Nick Birkett, marketing director at Stone King LLP

'I have received nothing but positive feedback from colleagues on the sessions Doug has run; he achieves great levels of engagement, he is straight talking, highly credible, and empathetic. He is able to focus people to a plan that they are bought into and motivated to deliver. One of the reasons he is able to achieve this is because he is so obviously genuine, and the fact he really cares shines through.'
Neil Cormack, head of business development and marketing at Lupton Fawcett Denison Till

'Doug is exactly what we needed to help us create more of a "sales" culture within the firm. His one-to-one sessions with some of our team have proved invaluable in kick-starting their BD activities and his focus on achieving results has paid dividends.

Doug is a straight talker, and although diplomatic, he rarely sugar-coats what needs to be said. A true professional and a nice guy too.'

Jason Edge, head of marketing and business development at Mayo Wynne Baxter Solicitors

The Visible Lawyer:
How to Raise Your Profile and Generate Work

DOUGLAS MCPHERSON

Head of legal publishing
Fiona Fleming

Publisher
Helen Donegan

Editor
Laura Slater

Published by ARK Group:

UK, Europe and Asia office
6–14 Underwood Street
London, N1 7JQ
United Kingdom
Tel: +44(0) 207 566 5792
publishing@ark-group.com

North America office
4408 N. Rockwood Drive, Suite 150
Peoria IL 61614
United States
Tel: +1 (309) 495 2853
publishingna@ark-group.com

www.ark-group.com

Printed by Canon (UK) Ltd, Cockshot Hill, Reigate, RH2 8BF, United Kingdom

ISBN: 978-1-78358-236-5

A catalogue record for this book is available from the British Library

ARK Group is a division of Wilmington plc. The company is registered in England &
Wales with company number 2931372 GB. Registered office: 6–14 Underwood Street,
London N1 7JQ. VAT Number: GB 899 3725 51.

Contents

Executive summary

Introduction – What is The Visible Lawyer?

'Marketing', 'business development', and (dare I sully the page) 'selling' are terms that are constantly redefined, reinvented, misused, and maligned in equal measure by the legal profession – to the point that all of these terms now have a different meaning to every lawyer in every law firm in every country. However, the truth of the matter is you could drop all of these terms tomorrow and replace them with a single word – 'visibility' – and the context in which they are used and the outcome they are designed to achieve will not alter in the slightest.

That is the idea behind *The Visible Lawyer*. Visibility is central to all of the themes, ideas, and suggestions covered in this book. Visibility is also central to your future success as a lawyer, irrespective of whether you are a solicitor or barrister in the UK or an attorney at law in the US, and whether you are newly qualified or an experienced partner.

If you are going to generate the maximum level of return from the limited time you as a lawyer have for marketing/business development/selling, then visibility must be your primary objective. You need to become a very visible lawyer.

In the coming chapters, we will look at visibility from every angle: where you need to be visible; how to achieve and, more importantly, maintain your visibility; and how to convert visibility into new work, whether the source of that work is new clients, your existing clients, or your professional contacts. You will also find practical advice you can put into immediate action.

All of the examples in the book are taken directly from my experience of working with solicitors, barristers, accountants, and IP attorneys across Europe, and all have proven to be successful in a professional services environment.

If working with law firms of all sizes has taught me one thing, that one thing would be that you did not enter the law to 'do' marketing, or business development, or selling; it is an add-on to your 'day job', and not always the most welcome one at that. However, the truth is that marketing and business development has never been as important as it is today. From a personal point of view, your career progression depends on your ability to generate work. From your firm's point of view, increased competition and increasingly discerning and promiscuous clients mean that unless every fee earner is prepared to contribute to winning work, the chance of building a successful and profitable future will diminish.

Being technically good and sitting by the phone while work finds you is no longer an option; you need to up your game. But the good news is there is a raft of different options you can employ to help you become more visible so you stay best placed as opportunities arise.

Within the professional services, the default reaction is often that 'marketing' means 'networking', which means formal networking *events,* and for many – me included – that type of event is hugely unattractive. *The Visible Lawyer* takes into account that, while the legal profession may not be heavily populated by natural salespeople, everyone involved has different skills, different personalities, and different preferences that they can put into action to generate visibility, for themselves, their firm, and for their colleagues.

I know that not all of the suggestions will suit you, but there are enough options outlined in these pages to ensure you will definitely find a few that do. Better still, if you are able to take on those ideas and implement them, your visibility will not only create opportunities but will also negate the need to 'sell' or 'close'. Being consistently visible will help you build effective interpersonal relationships that will lead to clients and referrers recognising you as the right person for the job, both technically and personally. As a result, these people will come to you to ask you to take on work, rather than forcing you to sell your services as one of a number of possible suppliers.

I also recognise that you have limited time to invest in creating visibility, which is why every idea in this book is designed to be implemented on a 'little and often' basis. All of the ideas can be put into practice around your fee-earning responsibilities so that the ubiquitous grumble of 'I'm too busy' can finally be kicked squarely into touch.

What does this book cover?

Part One of this book (Chapters 1–2), focuses on the theory of visibility: the foundation on which this book is built. Chapter 1 looks at where you need to be visible, who you want to be visible to, and how you turn all of that information into an easy-to-follow roadmap that will lead you to the clients and the work you want.

Chapter 2 describes how you can achieve a consistency of visibility by applying the rule of 'little and often'. It asks how you build visibility in the face of billing and client pressure, how you mix and match the various options available to create visibility, and what you can say and do to make sure the visibility you create translates into interest.

Part Two (Chapters 3–6) moves on to how you create visibility in practical terms. Chapter 3 considers 'intelligent marketing'; that is marketing that creates visibility. We look at the difference between intelligent and effective marketing and tick-box marketing, and the proven three-step 'intelligent marketing' model (Confidence, Focus, Action). This chapter shares some low-cost/high-impact business development strategies that really work, and practical tips to manage your marketing activities on a day-to-day basis.

Chapter 4 provides guidance to help you *stay visible* to current clients and leverage your existing relationships. It explains why you should change your mantra from 'client management' to 'client development' and outlines effective client development strategies.

Chapter 5 shifts the focus from clients to another essential group you need to stay visible to: referrers. This chapter explains why referrers and other industry contacts are as valuable as clients. It looks at how to build a referrer relationship model that really works, how you can grow your professional network, and how you can convert your relationships into work.

Chapter 6 provides actionable guidance on creating the visibility that wins new clients, including choosing the business development strategies that are best suited to you and how you leverage those strategies to create a personal BD plan that delivers. This chapter also explains how focusing on recognised industry groups or more defined geographies will help you generate the best return from the limited time and resources you have available.

Part Three of the book comprises a series of 'mini-masterclasses' with practical exercises that will help you craft your own visibility plan. Mini-masterclass 1 focuses on how to really network effectively: how to choose the right events and then achieve the best return on time invested in attending them, how to follow up, and how to stay in touch to maximise the likelihood that introductions will turn into instructions. The masterclass also considers the alternatives to formal networking events and how your more left-field contacts can help you build your professional network.

The second mini-masterclass focuses on how you can deliver presentations that create visibility by engaging your audiences. It addresses why public speaking is arguably the most effective BD strategy and which speaking platforms are available to you. It provides tips on creating and delivering presentations that really engage an audience, and explores how you can follow up on presentations to capitalise on the visibility you have created.

Mini-masterclass 3 covers how you can build visibility and profile through the written word. It asks which media will have the most impact, how you can harness the benefits of local, trade, and online publications, and what writing style and content will engage and benefit your target audience most.

Mini-masterclass 4 is your PR toolkit. This masterclass is guest-written by Sharon Cain, managing director at Quest PR, who steps in to help you to create an integrated PR and social media programme that will position you as a thought leader.

In the last of the mini-masterclasses, we examine the hugely valuable contribution research can make to your firm's business development activities, and how you can maximise the impact of the research you or your team undertake.

What gets measured is what gets done – and this also applies to your visibility plan. In light of this home truth, the final chapter of this book considers how to set personal objectives, how to make those objectives achievable, how to create personal templates that manage and record activity, and how best to publicise your success internally.

About the author

After graduating in marketing and post-graduating in advertising, Douglas went into sales thinking that if he could sell he'd never be out of work. Although it was meant to be a temporary step – a purely education-finishing assignment – he has never looked back.

His association with the professional services began in 1994 when he joined Intellectual Property Publishing where he soon became sales manager of the IP portfolio, and ultimately sales and marketing manager for the owning group, Armstrong.

When Armstrong was sold to Lloyd's of London Press, Douglas was promoted to commercial director of the Lloyd's Marine Intelligence Unit with full responsibility for promoting, packaging, and selling Lloyd's of London's market-leading shipping data output. This role saw him continue to work closely with the professional services, most notably the international Admiralty Law, marine underwriting, and marine finance and actuarial sectors, across the world's major shipping centres.

In 2010, Douglas joined Bernard Savage at Size 10½ Boots, a business development agency that works solely with the professional services, helping professionals to win more new clients and more work from the clients they already have.

The tips, tricks, and shortcuts in *The Visible Lawyer* are the result of a combination of Size 10½ Boots' partners' corporate and professional services experience and the no-nonsense, plain speaking, straightforward approach they have developed alongside their constantly growing client list.

Because of the nature of self-employment, there is never a lot of spare time, but any time Douglas does have is spent with family, coaching youth football, collecting obscure soul records, and swearing profusely at Chelsea Football Club.

Dedication

This book is dedicated to Claire, Daniel, and Harry who are always so patient with and accepting of the fact that I'm more than regularly miles away (physically and/or mentally) trying to help the solicitors, barristers, IP attorneys, and accountants we work with to get more visible. And to Frank Lampard. Because I can.

Part 1:
The theory of visibility

Chapter 1:
Where do you need to be visible?

Before you can take steps to become more visible, you need to know where you need to be visible and, more importantly, who you need to be visible to. If you are to work that out, you need to start by asking yourself one simple question: who do I want as clients? There are a number of filters you can apply in order to help you answer this question accurately and effectively. These include:

1. Your current client base

Which of your current clients do you genuinely like working with? Make a shortlist, then take a few minutes out to think about exactly why you like working with them. It may be that they are a similar age to you or from a similar background. It may be that their legal requirements are a little off-centre and therefore the work is more challenging and, by extension, more enjoyable. It may be because their business or their interests are related to a sector you are particularly interested in, common ground which makes spending time with them more pleasurable. Although there are myriad factors that could come out of this exercise, the one thing I can guarantee is that there will be some common themes.

2. Sectors of interest

Are there any industries or groups of individuals that really interest you? If yours is a commercial practice area, for example, it may be retail, sports, food and drink, or games and apps. If yours is a private client sector, it may be that you have a leaning towards particular nationalities, locations, or social demographics. As with all things in life, if you focus in on something you like and find interesting, any extra work required to crack that particular nut will be less of a chore and more likely to happen.

3. Sectors with opportunity

If your drivers are more financially based, there may be some potential client bases that offer more in terms of potential growth and opportunity than others. For example, the aforementioned games and apps sector is one that looks set to continue to grow on the commercial side. Similarly, more traditional industries like oil and gas may have started to decline, but under the energy umbrella there are new possibilities such as clean tech, and renewables continue to develop and take their place. Meanwhile, on the private client side, a number of professional services firms in the UK have reacted to the continued influx of Chinese nationals by building dedicated Chinese teams.

Building brand cameos

Once you have your common themes, you will have the DNA of your ideal client. We call this a 'brand cameo'. When you have a brand cameo, you will not only be able to go online and actually identify some potential targets, you will also be able to piece together some of their likely behaviours:

- Where do they congregate?
- What do they like to do?
- What do they read?
- Which events/conferences/exhibitions do they attend?
- Which other professionals (accountants, wealth managers, IP attorneys, IFAs) advise them?

With this insight, you can work out how best to reach them. You can go to the places and events they're likely to be at and 'engineer serendipity' by accidentally bumping into them on purpose. You can start to court editorial opportunities in their preferred publications. You can participate in the discussions they're having online and via social media. You can start to become *visible* to them.

Better still, because you have identified the common traits of your ideal clients, the routes to making yourself visible to those prospects will potentially make you visible to everyone who fits that cameo, not just to one specific target. This means that your marketing and business development is much more likely to actually achieve what should be your primary objective – generating new work.

'Yummy mummies', 'Academics', and 'Affluent greys'

Size 10½ Boots worked with a small regional firm in the UK who wanted to pursue the high net worth market, but they quickly realised such a well-worn and poorly defined grouping was far too woolly if they were going to build an effective marketing strategy around it.

Instead, they started to think a little more creatively and built more focused brand cameos. They carefully considered where each of those groups would congregate and, therefore, what the best communication routes to those different settings would be. The groups and routes they chose were:

- 'Yummy mummies' who hang about in fancy hair salons and coffee shops, and do what ladies of leisure do – go to the gym, and attend the various Ladies Clubs being run locally;

- 'Academics' who in the main lived in different parts of this particular university town and were definitely not turned on by champagne, glitz, and glamour, but instead wanted a more professional, service-driven offering; and

- 'Affluent greys' who lived and socialised in very different post codes again and had a very particular set of legal requirements given their level of wealth and stage of life.

The result of taking this more targeted approach was that the messages being put out were more relevant and more memorable, which made them more effective. Because those messages were then delivered through the means most likely to hit their targets, the firm quickly noticed they were not only achieving their primary objective – more work – but also seeing a reduction in their overall marketing spend.

Building brand cameos into an effective personal visibility plan

So, now you have an outline of the clients you want and a fairly accurate insight into their likely personal and/or professional behaviour. You now need to turn this into a plan that will bring you to their attention by utilising the available promotional vehicles.

When you sit down to build your personal visibility plan, the first thing to bear in mind is that you are most definitely not a full-time sales person (nor, I'm guessing, do you want to be), so the activities you choose have to be manageable alongside your fee-earning responsibilities.

When it comes to setting out plans, you are probably already aware of the acronym SMART (specific, measurable, achievable, realistic, and time-scaled). While I wouldn't say you need to follow this structure rigidly, it does provide a good mental tick-list to go through after you set your objectives, because if your plan ticks all of those boxes it will be much more likely to succeed. This is because it will be clear, and you will know:

- Exactly what needs to be achieved (specific);
- Exactly how many times you need to do it (measurable);
- Exactly why you're doing it and how you're going to do it (achievable);
- Exactly what you'll need to do it in terms of time, budget, and additional resources (realistic); and
- Exactly when you need to do it by (time-scaled).

You also need to be mindful of what you are actually good at, and what you will actually be comfortable delivering. If you choose a range of activities you don't like doing, then the chance you'll actually do them reduces, while the likelihood of your finding a reason not to do them increases. However, if you play to your strengths, you will not only be more likely to do what you set out to do, you will actually do it better. Why? Because you will be more confident, more comfortable, more genuine, and therefore more engaging.

And remember, everything you do marketing-wise – from speaking at an international conference down to updating your firm's blog – is in the shop window. If those looking through that window can sense what you're doing is either half-hearted or forced, they will not be impressed by or attracted to you so the majority of your efforts will be in vain.

To simplify the various options open to you, I will break things down into four groups – networkers, speakers, writers, and researchers – and while we will look at the practicalities of each of these in much more detail in the mini-masterclasses later in the book, here is a brief introduction to each:

1. Networkers

When it comes to marketing legal services, there is an incorrect assumption that by 'marketing' we (the marketing and BD community) mean 'networking', and that by 'networking' we mean formal networking events.

It's true that traditional networking will be involved in some shape or form, but you should only include it within your plan if you are going to approach it seriously. If networking is going to be productive, you need to go to every event so that you start to build trust within the group.

You also need to totally forgo the 'went once, didn't get any work, won't go again' mind-set. You need to go in full 'I want to meet you' mode and make sure you put yourself about, talk to as many people as you can, and then follow up properly.

You also need to be patient. Once you are immersed in a particular network, you will receive referrals that convert quickly, but attaining that positon may take a while. Again, you have to adopt a mind-set that blocks out 'went once, didn't get any work, won't go again'.

Networking events are a fantastic and proven way of making new contacts, but there are other types of networking out there. You can arrange to meet smaller groups in the pub, get a few contacts with a shared interest together, visit clients and spend some time chatting to them about things other than the matter at hand; you can join sports or personal interest clubs, you can volunteer to join local committees or relevant trade associations, you can even just plan to make more of social events.

My business partner, Bernard Savage, and I have won work from chatting to a fellow parent who turned out to be a lawyer, who – after following up with an invitation for a beer – referred us to a patent attorney he knew. We also won an opportunity for a client to deliver a seminar to a group at the heart of their target market on the back of a chat with a fellow parent at an under-12s football match.

Closer to home, our agency, Size 10½ Boots, wouldn't exist if I hadn't chatted to the enthusiastic stranger who struck up a conversation with me one sunny afternoon at Nottingham Castle.

Thinking on your feet in the gym

A few days after a networking training session, a senior family partner in Lincolnshire found herself at her local gym in unexpected conversation with a particularly chatty chap she hadn't met before.

By her own admission, her usual reaction would be to make a few polite noises and then gently excuse herself as quickly as possible. However, because her recent training was front of mind, she thought 'you never know' and decided to make an effort to see what happened next.

Having taken time to listen to the man and take an interest in who he was and what he did, she was given the opportunity to tell him what she did. He then told her about his previous divorce and how poor his lawyer had been throughout the process, itself a catalogue of disasters that had them both laughing out loud.

A few days later, he turned up in the partner's waiting room and instructed her on his second and somewhat lucrative separation.

2. Speakers

While networking is a proven way to meet people, statistically the most effective way to build visibility is to be the speaker at the event.

If you think about the maths, if you go to a networking event with 60 guests, you may speak to six people. Of those, three may be of professional interest and worthy of meaningful follow-up (i.e. getting together for a coffee – you should always follow up with an email and LinkedIn request). That is only 5 per cent of the attendees.

If you are the key note speaker, you speak to *everybody* present. More than that, you underline your credentials as the 'go to' person in your field for all of those in attendance. Better still, a large percentage of those are likely to come up to you to give you a card or ask for a copy of your slides – and they wouldn't do that unless they were interested in what you had to say, which means all are either potential clients or introducers (as long as you follow up and stay visible, of course).

In order to use speaking platforms to build visibility, broadly speaking there are two options. You can speak at third-party events, or you can organise and run your own seminars (though it's important to bear in mind the traditional seminar is losing popularity in an age where information is more freely available than ever). In Mini-masterclass 2 we will look in more detail at how to identify and pursue the right third party opportunities and at some more contemporary and more creative seminar models.

3. Writers

Having said that the increased volume of information available today is a threat to speaking, it is however an opportunity when it comes to writing. All of that information has to come from somewhere and be published somewhere by someone.

When it comes to writing, there are a number of options. You can blog, you can write articles, and you can write shorter opinion pieces. You can write for established trade and/or local publications or you can self-publish special reports and white papers or a client newsletter that brings together all of your content for your clients and contacts.

Again, we will look at how to use all of these options to create visibility in more detail in Mini-masterclass 3. We will also look at how to get the greatest possible return from everything you write as well as how to work out what to write about and how best to convey the points you wish to make.

4. Researchers

While you should be engaged in at least one (but preferably more) of the three previous activities, if the idea of marketing and business development really does bring you out in a cold sweat then there is a fourth option: research.

The networkers in your team or at your firm need to know where to go. Similarly, your writers need to know where to write and your speakers where to speak. One of the most often overlooked tasks in business development is research, yet it does make a valuable contribution to your firm or department's marketing efforts.

It's worth noting that, though it does add value to the overall marketing effort, in terms of creating personal visibility, research is not the most productive mechanism. That said, if you are to find the most productive events, networks, speaking platforms, and publications in terms of getting in front of your chosen targets, it is a useful skill to have so we will be looking at desk research in more detail in Mini-masterclass 5.

Choosing the most productive marketing options for you

Nobody knows you better than you. Take some time to think about the various options open to you and which you feel you are best suited to (referring to the relevant chapters for more detail is probably a good idea before you come to a final decision).

There is a view in some quarters that lawyers should push themselves 'out of their comfort zone' and get involved in the activities they are less comfortable with as part of their personal development. I don't subscribe to that view. I think you are far better to concentrate on the things you are naturally good at and do them better, do them more often, do them more efficiently, and do them in a more focused way.

The reason I think that way comes back to the idea that all of this stuff ('stuff' being the technical term for marketing initiatives and activities!) happens in the shop window. I know 'you don't get a second chance to make a first impression' is a cliché, but it only became a cliché because it's true.

Make sure that everything you do to push your personal visibility makes a positive impression on the people you are becoming more visible to by doing it well and doing it enthusiastically. In the main, people want two things from a potential professional adviser: confidence and likeability. If you are nervous in yourself or in your subject matter, you will promote neither, and the likelihood you'll get a second opportunity to try to create either with a particular person is negligible.

That means that when it comes to shortlisting your preferred routes to market, you need to be realistic and disciplined. Choose which of the four activities you want to use and then jot down how you want to use them next to the heading.

For example, if I were to do this exercise, my results would look something like Table 1.

Heading	Activity
Networking	Continue informal beers in various cities across UK Continue quarterly client lunches with banking contacts Ask for introductions from accountancy clients Ask for introductions from IP clients
Speaking	No thank you!
Writing	Continue column for Solicitors Journal Continue column for Private Client Adviser Write *Tenandahalf* blog LinkedIn postings Maintain presence in other legal publications I've previously written for
Research	Find new legal publications Continue to research the law firms that meet our preferred brand cameo and identify potential introductions

Table 1: Plotting your best route to market

What do you know now?

If you've followed each step (as illustrated in Figure 1), you will now have a mental or physical list that covers:

- Who you want to get visible to;
- How you could get visible to them; and
- How you will get visible to them.

This is your personal business development plan. What you need to do now is to add in the SMART aspect so that you can implement that plan in a consistent and meaningful way so that you start to build visibility. This is exactly what we'll be looking at in Chapter 2.

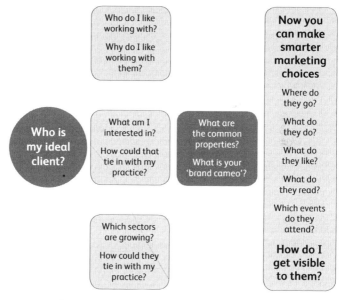

Figure 1: Where do you want to be visible – and to whom?

Chapter 2:
How do you achieve a consistency of visibility?

In the last chapter, we looked at how to build a personal business development plan based upon:

- The clients you want; and
- The methods you want to use to make sure you become visible to your chosen targets.

Now that you have your plan, you need to make sure its implementation is successful. If I may, I'd like to go back to my time as a marketing undergraduate. Although this was much further back in time than I'd care to admit, there is one lecture I remember clearly (and repeatedly use as an example) to this day. It was an interview with the then UK marketing director of Coca-Cola.

The crux of the interview was that Coca-Cola didn't advertise everywhere (from national TV right down to the awning outside and fridge front inside your local newsagent) and sponsor everything (from international sporting events to local community events) to sell cans of drink. They did it so that when consumers were thirsty, they thought of Coca-Cola. This is one of the world's largest corporations and arguably the world's largest brand embodying the very essence of the theory of visibility.

Obviously, you have nothing like the resources of Coca-Cola at your disposal, but wherever you're based and whichever practice area you work in, the lesson is just as valid. Your success is not just about achieving visibility, it is also about *maintaining* your visibility.

I often say that you can't make someone instruct you, but you can stack the odds in your favour. Just as the blanket advertising, sponsorship, and branding employed by Coca-Cola was intended to keep their name front of mind in case a consumer wanted a can of pop, you need to make sure that whenever your clients, contacts, and targets need your services, you are front of mind. This means that you need to achieve a level of consistency in your marketing.

We see far too many lawyers dropping their marketing efforts when they're busy and then filling in the quiet times with either a few token gestures or a panic-driven marketing frenzy. Neither approach will work, for three key reasons: statistics; human nature; and competition.

1. Statistics
The likelihood that the person you are speaking to will need the services you provide at the exact time you've chosen to pull yourself away from your desk to speak to them is skeletal (never mind thin). You will get lucky (and we will come back to how you can make your own luck) occasionally, but it doesn't happen often – and it certainly doesn't happen if you only apply yourself to business development in fits and starts.

2. Human nature
How would you feel if you had a contact that only got in touch sporadically, and then only when they needed something? Worse still, how would you feel if it was *patently obvious* they were only getting in touch sporadically and when they needed something? Winning work comes down to establishing productive, mutually beneficial relationships – and that type of relationship can only be established when contact is consistent.

3. Competition
Leaving huge gaps in your business development only plays into the hands of one group: your competitors. Just as you are under pressure to 'get out there', so too are your competitors. While

the two bands most at risk from your competitors' attentions are your professional contacts and your targets, don't be fooled into thinking your clients aren't also at risk. Client relationships are all about service, and if your clients sense a slip in service (or accessibility and responsiveness) and your competitors hit them at just the right time, those relationships could be damaged.

Little and often

So, given that you have got to do the work, that you only have a certain amount of time to do that work, and that clients always have to come first, what's the answer? The short answer is: 'little and often'. Yet again, this is a cliché; but yet again, it's a cliché that's only found its way into common parlance because it's absolutely true.

In the legal profession, marketing doesn't have to mean a time-consuming lunch, a conference that requires a full week out of the office, or a seminar that takes you two days to research, a day to write, and a day to deliver. Here are some time-efficient alternatives you can employ easily alongside delivering your billable targets (even in the busiest times):

1. (Personalised) 'saw this and thought of you' emails

If you are truly immersed in your sector (whether that sector is defined by standard industry classification or by geography) you will know what's going on within it. Some of this intelligence will come from conversations, but some of it should also be coming from open sources (e.g. Google alerts, RSS feeds from the relevant publications and websites and from social media. I know it's a bit 'old school', but you can even use newspapers and magazines.)

As these arrive and strike a chord with recent matters and your knowledge of client requirements, be prepared to cut and paste (or cut them out if you – like me – are still old school) and send them to those you know will be interested. I can honestly say, however clever we think we're being with our own marketing, these messages are the ones that generate the most goodwill and, by extension, the best response.

2. (Mass) 'saw this and thought of you' emails

Basically as above, but if you're:

a.   Organised;

b.   Have a good relationship with your marketing people; and

c.   Have the right software;

you can send the same message to a group comprising all of the relevant contacts in seconds, saving you the time it would take to send the same thing out on an individual basis to every relevant party.

3. Making better use of key industry/local events

As we'll come onto in the networking mini-masterclass later in the book, 'events' doesn't (and shouldn't) just mean the obvious choices – for example, in the UK, Chamber or IoD events. These will be swamped with your competitors and the likelihood of meeting anyone a) useful or b) new is slim.

I'm not denigrating this type of event in any way. If you can make them work for you – and many lawyers can, thanks to hard graft, consistency, and commitment – then that's great. What I am saying is that there are rafts of other events locally that have been specifically designed to service your sector or your geography. If you can find these, you will find you could be one of the only lawyers in the room. You will also find you will see a number of existing contacts and new prospective clients and/or referrers in one hit.

The events are usually run monthly and outside office hours. That means if you could commit to attending 10 during the year, you will have the ability to connect with and stay visible to a range of potentially useful contacts in return for giving up 20 hours that in all probability wouldn't be billed anyway.

4. Four-ball lunches

It doesn't take a genius to work out that seeing three people at once is more time efficient than seeing those three people separately. It's also not a huge leap to recognise that a conversation involving four will be wider and more fluid than a conversation between two people.

This is why the 'four-ball' is one of the most effective marketing tools at your disposal. If you could commit to hosting one per quarter, you will see 12 key contacts during the year and get to spend quality social time with them while doing them a favour.

That feeling that you're doing your guests a favour is the real benefit of the 'four-ball'; it cannot fail to generate positive PR for you. If you choose your guests carefully, each should be able to help the other guests in some capacity so people will start to regard you as someone that makes things happen – the 'go to' person in your particular area. This alone will increase your referral rate.

5. LinkedIn on the move

I'm not sure what your journey to work is like, but for many it is 'dead time'. It's too short (and public) to do anything meaningful work-wise, but it is by definition an unavoidable chore and time commitment none of us can get out of.

This is where smart phones come into their own. Even in its new (and hopefully soon to be changed incarnation), LinkedIn offers a really easy memory-jog. If you can scroll through when you have a spare five minutes, you will soon spot those you haven't seen for a while and probably really should see soon.

Better still, there's a direct message function that means that as soon as you can see someone you haven't – but should have – been in contact with, you can drop them a line to ask if they're OK and if they fancy a coffee or a sandwich.

Some fee earners think this is a little intrusive, but the truth is that whichever study you read, the results will show categorically that people like seeing a red flag on their phone's screen. People are flattered you've chosen to get in contact and are more likely to respond positively to an approach made via social media than they are to an approach made to their email address.

6. '10 before 10'

One of the best personal marketing initiatives I have come across is the '10 before 10'. Basically, you choose a day (Wednesday was the day of choice for my client) and say to yourself: 'On that day I'm going to make 10 calls to clients/contacts/targets before 10am.'

In the case of my client, what he said on those calls depended on the person he was calling. It might have been a 'How's it going?' call (clients); it may have been a 'Must have a coffee' call (contacts); or it may have been an 'I'd like to ask you for lunch' call (target). It was, it must be said, rare that he ever got to 10 as the first five calls usually filled the hour he'd set aside.

The moral of the story is that he took one solitary hour out of his working week, dedicated himself to the task at hand, and generated enough meetings to keep his pipeline (direct and introductions) full enough to eschew any other marketing activities.

The 'marketing mix'

One of the first principles you learn when you study marketing is that of the 'marketing mix'. Although people much cleverer than me have defined and articulated this lofty concept, it boils down to one thing: you need to do a bit of everything because people respond to different things at different times and if you ignore a particular route to market or concentrate on only one type of activity, you'll never generate the best level of return.

Generally speaking, in a legal environment the best way of winning work is to stay visible to your clients, referrers, and contacts by spending time with them (again, fully utilising the 'little and often' mantra). However, in between those meetings you need to make sure you remain visible and don't slip off your contacts' radars.

This is where you need to think about what we very technically refer to as the 'in-betweeny-joiny-up-stuff'. This is where the marketing mix comes into its own. Thanks largely to the advent of the smartphone, it is now much easier for you to employ much more variety and creativity to make sure you stay visible in between face-to-face meetings so the meetings you're having are joined up into a consistent campaign, rather than being little more than a series of haphazard one-offs.

Better still (thanks again to the advent of the smart phone), all your supporting 'in-betweeny-joiny-up-stuff' requires for implementation is an investment of a few seconds. Here are a few options you could add to your personal marketing mix:

1. 'Saw this and thought of you'

Yes, again… but it works *so* well so I will keep banging the drum!

2. LinkedIn

It takes seconds to add an update but people do pick up on them, especially if you can inject a bit of humour and a bit of yourself. Postings admittedly take longer but they are – as I type at least – much more effective because a notification of their publication goes direct to all of your contacts. This means it acts like a mini-advertising campaign on your behalf while underlining your capabilities within a particular area related to your practice.

3. Twitter

Twitter causes some consternation for some lawyers so if you are one of those, discount this option now. If you are to build up the type of following that will create and maintain visibility, you need to be comfortable giving an opinion and creating conversations with people you have never met. You also need to be able to mix up the factual with the informal and be prepared to use a lighter touch than you normally would when you're doing your legal work. Similarly, although a tweet only takes a few seconds to write and send, you need to do it consistently. I have heard too many professionals say that Twitter is going to be a mainstay of their marketing plan and they are prepared to commit to one or two tweets per week. Wrong. You need to be sending, responding to, and engaging with tweets throughout the day if you're going to make this platform work for you.

Although it is – as with all professions – a mixed bag, generally speaking in the UK the group who are good at Twitter are barristers. Never shy of an opinion (or promoting it) they tend to be more forthright and more tongue in cheek than the majority of other lawyers or accountants. If you are interested in seeing their approach, I'd suggest looking at @Charonqc, @DefenceGirl, and (although he is a clerk rather than a barrister) @notabarrister as examples of tweeting best practice.

4. Newsletter contributions

Again, this is something we will look at in more detail later in the book, but the one thing I always say in defence of the much maligned law firm newsletter is, as with PowerPoint, just because people use it badly doesn't mean it's a bad thing. If your newsletter is short, punchy, relevant, and practical, it will be of value to the recipient; and if it is of value, people will keep it to refer to, and they will get in touch with you should they require more information.

Your newsletter also acts as a reminder that you're out there (again joining up contact in between meeting in person) and the fact that it puts your or your firm's name into the inbox of a contact is valuable in itself.

The content assembled for your newsletter also gives you more potential 'saw this and thought of yous'. If you – or one of your colleagues – have written something of relevance to one of your contacts, send it to them with a personal cover note. Again, thanks to the smart phone, the share function means you can do this in seconds, on the move, and outside of billable time.

And don't limit your sharing to your firm's newsletter; some of the accountants, IFAs, patent attorneys, chambers, surveyors, banks, agents you work with will also be producing content. If their content is of relevance to your clients, ask them if you can forward it (a personal visibility touchpoint in itself). Flattery alone will generate a positive response.

5. External columns

Again, we will come back to this in Mini-masterclass 3, but everything you produce for a third party (the local or trade press) can be sent out to contacts or can be added to your website so you can distribute the links via social media… or preferably both!

How do you turn visibility into interest?

Once you have created and maintained your visibility, what do you need to do to turn that visibility into interest? The way to do that is simple: you need to have something interesting to say.

From the off, you need to be able to say something that will resonate with your audience. You need to be able to underline not only your professional suitability (your technical ability, the relevance of your particular practice area), but also your personal suitability (that you are the type of person they'd like to work with and someone who will deliver the advice they require efficiently and with the required level of service).

Creating a solid and attractive client value proposition for your firm

In my opinion, too many firms have become overly concerned with trying to identify their point of differentiation or their unique selling points (USPs). Identifying these mythical beasts is often a time-consuming and expensive exercise. More worryingly, it is an exercise that forces meaningful visibility-building marketing activity into the background while a resolution all of the partners agree with is reached. I would also add that in the majority of cases the results I've seen are neither unique nor strong enough to achieve any level of differentiation and firms are often left saying the same thing as their competitors, albeit in slightly different words.

I strongly feel that instead of searching for unique or differentiating statements, law firms should instead concentrate their efforts on establishing a solid client value proposition (CVP). In marketing terms, a CVP consists of the sum total of benefits the firm promises their clients will enjoy in return for the fees they pay the firm. But if that sounds a bit like marketing gobbledygook, then a simpler way of looking at it is to imagine you've just met somebody for the very first time and they've asked: 'Why should I use you?'. You need to be able to come back with a succinct description of your firm and the services it provides. Moreover, you need to be able to demonstrate quickly and plainly why those services will benefit, rather than simply cost, the person you are talking to. It should make them want to buy your services and come to you when they need legal advice in any area.

If it is constructed correctly, your CVP will generate interest because it will encapsulate the good stuff you do and why that good stuff will help the person you're talking to achieve their desired outcome as quickly, efficiently, and cost-effectively as possible. More importantly, it will mark you out from the 'I'm a lawyer from a well-established firm that has x partners and y location and provides a full service legal offering covering all practice areas a business or individual will need' school of marketing. This is a line I have heard far too many times and it could never be considered a client value proposition because it is 100 per cent inwardly focused and proposes no tangible value for the client.

Instead, your CVP should focus on the key aspects of your service offering, irrespective of whether those components are current or aspirational. You then need to be able to explain why they're of value to clients, which means they need to be applicable to all of the areas of law your firm covers. If they cannot be applied to every practice area, your CVP will never be successfully implemented because, as with everything involved in a successful external marketing effort, consistency is key.

This doesn't mean your aim is to provide the dreaded 'elevator script', something cosmetic and insincere that every fee earner is expected to memorise and recite at will in any situation. We're not trying to produce an army of automaton salespeople. We are, however, looking to make sure that people get the same message from every touchpoint they have with your firm, so simplicity is essential.

Try to settle on two, three, or at the very most four key components. Once this list is agreed, ask yourself a simple question: *So what?* The answer to this question should articulate how/why/where that component will provide real benefit for your clients, referrers, and targets. It should be a personalised statement articulated in the right context that will allow you to build on the visibility you've created by making people interested in you and willing to continue the conversation, if not immediately, in the very near future.

Once you have your CVP, you need to integrate it within every client-facing channel you use. That list includes (but is definitely not limited to): in person; online; and in writing.

1. In person

You'd use it while networking (formally or informally), at the firm's social events, when you hold meetings, and when you are introduced to new people. However, it also needs to be launched properly so that every member of staff understands it. If you are boasting 'responsiveness and accessibility', you need to be responsive and accessible, all day every day and at all levels, otherwise your credibility will fall at the first hurdle.

2. Online

The concepts would be integrated into the copy on the 'Home' and 'About us' pages of your website, but again you need to make sure your design and navigation adheres to your principles. If you are 'straightforward and uncomplicated', your website and the copy you include on that site needs to be too!

3. In writing

Your articles and blogs and your newsletters need to live up to your claims. If you are 'plain speaking' but send out nothing but overly long and impenetrable technical legal opinions, you'll lose ground. Similarly, if you are 'completely cutting edge' but don't comment on a major story in your main areas for several weeks, you won't be taken seriously.

Your brochures and formal tender submissions should also make mention of your CVP because the sole purpose of those vehicles is to make people want to buy their legal advice from you, which means they need to clearly (and consistently) set out the benefits the client will enjoy should they do so.

Creating a personal value proposition

As I've said, your CVP is not an elevator script so you need to be able to articulate it in a way that is relevant to your practice area and to your client base (whether those clients are existing, lapsed, or prospective). Sometimes, this is as simple as changing the word 'business' to 'you and your family', but sometimes it can be more involved. Look at the core concepts of your firm's CVP and think about your clients and their needs, and how your advice delivers against those needs.

For example, if one of your core concepts is protecting your clients, 'protection' could mean:

- If you are an IP/IT lawyer – Protecting the client's brand and ideas so that they are not commercially abused by competitors;

- If you are a commercial lawyer – Protecting a company's best interests and ensuring the safest possible environment in which to trade by providing robust Ts and Cs and contracts;

- If you are a private client lawyer – Protecting a client's assets and wealth and making it as tax efficient as possible so that their family enjoys the maximum financial benefit in the future;

- If you are a corporate lawyer – Protecting the client's best interests during a purchase or disposal so that the deal delivers the best possible return at the best possible price for your client; or

- If you are an employment lawyer – Protecting the business against unnecessary expensive, drawn out, and stressful claims tribunals.

The second bit is to think about how you introduce yourself so that what you do for a living appears to be valuable and interesting. I know you've trained hard to get to where you are but 'I'm a corporate lawyer' probably won't create the buzz at the dinner table you think it should. Many people won't know the difference between the different practice areas (if that is the prefix you use) and will only hear 'lawyer'. You need to say something that echoes with what people need and, gently, injects a little humour so that you start to mark yourself out from your competitors as someone they could possibly work with in the future.

One of the best examples of the opening gambit that I have ever heard was from a tax manager at a small firm of accountants in North London. She came into her personal coaching session complaining that many people switched off when she said she was a tax accountant (or switched off once she explained, at their request, what a tax manager actually was) and she wasn't getting anywhere, despite investing a lot of her own time in networking.

I asked her what she really did and her reply was: 'I stop people paying any more tax than they need to.' That was perfect (it certainly resonated with me) so, from that moment on, instead of opening with 'I'm a tax manager', the lady opened with: 'You know you hate paying tax? Well it's my job to make sure you never pay more than you have to.'

The reversal in her fortunes was immediate. People started to laugh and immediately recognised that her services did add value, which gave her a reason to meet again, one-on-one, after the event and start building a relationship with the new contacts she was now making.

As an aside, she also saw an increase in personal referrals because her contacts recognised exactly how she could add value to the people within their networks and recognised exactly when to drop her name into the conversation.

How do you make sure your (firm's or personal) value proposition is in line with what your clients want?

This is the easy part: you ask them. For some reason, lawyers often feel awkward asking clients for feedback. Typically, they restrict the feedback process to impersonal questionnaires which deliver little value due to the fact they are only completed by people who have either found working with you an extremely positive experience or an extremely negative one. However, the truth is that people are always flattered to be asked for their perspective, mainly because they want to put over their opinions but also, more subliminally, because they know that their feedback will improve the quality of service they receive in the future.

In terms of getting feedback on your client value proposition, there are two ways this can be done:

- You can drop it into a formal client service review; and
- You can drop it in at the end of a more informal meeting.

First, you'll need to explain the context. You've been doing some work on the way you present your services and would like to see if you're on the right lines. Then explain the proposition you've arrived at and ask if that fits a) with their expectations of a legal services provider and b) is something they think would attract them to a specific legal services provider.

In almost every case, your client/contact/target will agree with what you put forward, but if they offer amendments acknowledge them, thank your contact for their suggestions, and then use them to refine your proposition, even if those refinements are minor.

Human nature sometimes makes it difficult for us to accept constructive criticism when we've worked hard on something, but remember the people you are asking are the people who do/would/should buy your services so, in this context, they actually do know better.

The other thing is asking for this type of feedback gives you a perfect reason to get in front of the contact or client in question, which gives you another way to – you've guessed it – *increase your visibility.*

Part 2:
Visibility in practice – How do you create visibility?

Chapter 3:
'Intelligent marketing' –
Practical marketing activities
that really do create visibility

What is 'intelligent marketing'?

One of the words we will keep coming back to in this book is 'practical': all of the marketing you do has to be practical and straightforward to implement. One of the themes we will keep coming back to is cost-efficiency; you do not have a corporate marketing budget at your disposal so you need to make sure every pound you are able to spend delivers a return, whether that return is financial or simply added visibility in the target market(s) you have chosen.

At Size 10½ Boots, we've married practicality and cost-efficiency under the umbrella of 'intelligent marketing'. What we mean by intelligent marketing is that, given your limited time and resources and the fact you are under pressure to deliver billable hours, you (as an intelligent professional) need to focus on marketing activities that actually work, the activities that are repeatedly proven to create visibility in a legal services context.

Intelligent marketing also allows you to fulfil your second objective: to deliver a return whilst keeping your head of department/managing partner/financial director happy.

The types of activities we are talking about are low cost, but high impact. They do not require generous or elastic budgets; in fact, I would strongly suggest that the traditional, expensive mass-appeal marketing techniques no longer work in the vast majority of cases.

What we are talking about here is doing stuff that works a lot, not stuff that costs a lot.

What is the difference between 'intelligent marketing' and 'tick-box marketing'?

What is 'tick-box' marketing? The easiest way to describe it is: the process of doing the same old things you always have marketing-wise because you know you need to do *something*.

These activities tend to be expensive (advertising, sponsorship, golf days, large-scale hospitality), but more damagingly, they are also often unproven because they have been running so long no one actually measures the return each initiative delivers. The difference between 'intelligent' and 'tick-box marketing' comes down to cost and return, both of which are crucial to the construction of a commercially viable business development model.

As I have said before, you only have limited time, budget, and resources at your disposal, so you need to make sure you get the best possible return from all three. This means you need to stretch yourself and your money tight across the activities you know will create visibility, rather than just throw what you have at grandiose marketing gestures.

Get off the roundabout and into the community

One mid-tier firm on the south coast used a large portion of their annual marketing budget to sponsor a local roundabout. When we asked the partners why they did this, one told us that it was a strong brand awareness tool. People knew the roundabout and the local radio station actually referred to it as [insert the firm's name] roundabout in morning travel bulletins, which proved it *had* to be a great brand awareness tool.

The only problem was nobody could remember the last time a client matter was opened as a result of someone having seen their logo on the roundabout or, for that matter, because someone had caught the firm's name during a traffic bulletin.

As the bulk of the practice was focused on services for individuals, we agreed a replacement strategy. Instead of using the roundabout, the firm re-appropriated their budget to fund their attendance at local community events like fetes, open days, and community group meetings. However, they didn't just attend; they rolled up their sleeves and got involved. They ran games and competitions that required visitors to start conversations with them (and to leave their contact details).

The result was that not only did they boost visibility within the epicentre of their target market – the local community – they also created warm leads they could follow up on comfortably. These leads converted in significantly higher numbers than ever before (due in no small part, I'm willing to bet, to the fact the conversations had been started in more personal and less stuffy circumstances).

However, there were other benefits too. Because they were seen to be genuinely interested in their community, further invitations came to run clinics at the local women's institute and yacht club, and to set up a pop-up shop once a month in the busiest bank in the area.

Farmers, commuters, and attention to detail

For one of the larger law firms in a South East England commuter town, the largest single marketing cost each year was a billboard at the town's railway station. The only trouble was, despite continual expensive contract renewals, it was not generating any results.

Part of this was down to the fact that the artwork had never been changed, only papered over with a new version of the same images and copy. Within the advertising industry there is a theory called 'print blindness' that says that if the same audience sees the same copy in the same place over time, they will eventually stop seeing it at all.

However, while 'print blindness' was undoubtedly a contributory factor, somewhat embarrassingly, the main reason that the firm was not receiving phone calls off the back of the billboard was that the proof had not been properly checked and the phone number given was actually incorrect.

Having agreed their two main targets – the town's more affluent commuter families and the region's farmers – the client released their billboard and redeployed the newly available budget into two key initiatives:

1. A 'coffee plan' that would bring them closer to the area's professionals and create referrals

The firm's fee earners identified the most productive of their professional contacts and created a target list of the professionals they knew were well regarded, but with whom the firm didn't already have existing relationships. They then worked out which fee earners would take responsibility for each of these, and they developed a contact plan designed to help them build visibility via one-on-one 'coffee' meetings, networking, social, and team-on-team events and, ultimately, joint marketing initiatives to their combined client bases.

2. A rural business plan that would make them more visible to not only the local farmers, but also to the wider commercial community that had built up in the rural areas surrounding the city

Recognising the rural community was exactly that – rural, the fee earners interested in building visibility within the farming sector used their existing client relationships to identify the key local events, for example the various agricultural shows and ploughing matches, which would bring them into contact with the farming community. Again, the emphasis was on participation not sponsorship and they designed a series of competitions for the visitors' children that allowed them to capture contact details and open conversations that could be followed up on. Meanwhile, they made a specific effort to start conversations with the other businesses supporting the events, all of which became targets for the commercial teams within the firm.

In the first year alone, the dual strategy created a wealth of new opportunities for both groups and the continuance of these initiatives has provided the firm with a platform from which to open a new office elsewhere in the county.

Ten low-cost/high-impact business development strategies that really work

In order to get you started on the road to visibility, here are 10 'intelligent marketing' initiatives that we not only know work but also see working, week in week out, during the course of our work with a huge number of national and regional professional services firms.

1. 'Don't sell, drink coffee'

However sophisticated and varied your personal business development plan becomes, the fact is the single most productive activity you will ever employ is spending time with people. With that in mind, you should skew the time you have for marketing towards coffee (or tea, beer, wine, organic juice, or antioxidant smoothies – 'coffee' is an umbrella term, not an instruction).

Increase the frequency with which you spend time with your key clients, contacts, and targets so that you stay visible to them and start to build the types of relationships that consistently generate new matters.

2. Participate in events, don't just attend them

While a speaking slot is always the ideal way to participate in the events most relevant to your practice, they do take time to secure and to prepare and are only a viable marketing option if you are truly comfortable speaking.

Whether you are the speaking type or not, you will need to attend events (whether those events are organised by your firm or a third party). If you are going to generate any benefit from your attendance, you will need to take an active part and not just hang around talking to the same people until you feel you've done your duty and can go home.

With any type of event, confidence is key. You need to be confident you have an attractive value proposition, confident you have something interesting to say. Most importantly, you have to have the confidence to realise everyone else in the room is in the same boat as you. They want someone to take the lead and start a conversation. If that someone is you, you will immediately stand out from those marking time by staring at their feet or their watches.

3. Follow up (quickly) after networking

Once you have met someone at an event, follow up. Make sure you show you are genuinely interested in getting your 'coffee' in first. All it takes is a quick email (the mini-masterclass on networking later in the book contains an email template you can cut and paste to speed the process up even further).

Remember, there are many reasons someone might not come back to you by return. Lack of response does not signify a lack of interest. They could have had an urgent piece of client work appear on their desk, they could be away from their desk in an internal meeting, they could just have missed your email in amongst the trials of their day.

Keep going: it's another cliché, but *persistence pays off.* On a more practical level, persistence will underline just how keen you are to progress your conversation, which will eventually nudge a response out of your target.

4. Get articles published

Having articles published is a good way to establish thought leadership credentials within an audience group you would not otherwise be able to influence. It also gives you the perfect ammunition to fuel your 'in-betweeny-joiny-up' efforts. Your publisher will provide you with a branded PDF that you can distribute via all of the marketing channels available to you – your social media feeds, your website, and as an e-shot to the relevant portions of your marketing database.

Again, we will come onto creating content in much more detail later in the book, but I'd like to end this short introduction with the golden rule: if you are going to create visibility in the right areas, you *must* get published in the titles your clients, contacts, and targets read, not in the publications you and your profession reads.

5. 'Saw this and thought of you'

Yes, *that* again!

6. Have a referral strategy

For too many lawyers, referrals are a bit haphazard. When they come it's nice, but there's not really any thought given to how they appeared or, indeed, how best to keep them coming.

If you know exactly what you want (your brand cameos, your ideal clients, the sectors or geography you want to pursue), you can have a think about who amongst the people you know could introduce you to your chosen targets.

Make a list of who you want to know, then run them through LinkedIn and when you see a mutual contact, ask that mutual contact to make an introduction. Some see this as pushy, but remember flattery is a powerful tool. People will be glad you have: a) recognised they are the mutual link; and b) that you think of them as someone well-connected enough to be able to bring that connection to life.

If you're still sceptical, give it a test. Start with one potential introduction that someone you know very well could make and ask them if they'll put you in touch. They'll say yes, then you can start to be more adventurous.

7. Gather case studies

Adding case studies to your website, to your marketing collateral, and to formal tender documents will bring your story to life. The trouble is, as soon as most people hear 'case study' they are immediately transported back to school or university and are seized by the fear that putting together a detailed case study takes enormous amounts of time, research, and elbow grease.

Let's dispel that myth right now. You can have a one paragraph case study, which can be written quickly and will actually stand a much better chance of being read and absorbed by the reader. This means they're not only easier to produce, but are also more likely to actually have a positive effect on your marketing efforts.

The structure I use for a short case study is CAR:

- **Context**: What situation was your client confronted with?
- **Action**: What did you do for your client to help them resolve the situation they faced?
- **Result**: What outcome did your intervention and action achieve for your client?

But keep it short; case studies are for generating interest, they're not meant to be a comprehensive course text.

8. Use LinkedIn little and often

LinkedIn is only going to grow in importance so you need to be taking full advantage of it. Take five minutes a day to keep up to date with where your contacts are and what they're saying.

It's called *social* media for a reason so take full advantage of the messaging function. Say happy birthday, acknowledge a new job or a job anniversary, and be confident enough to add an update a couple of times a week to tell people what you're up to.

One thing I have noticed when it comes to updates (and postings for that matter) on LinkedIn is it's the lighter touches that generate the highest return. Be prepared to say what *you* are doing, not always what the firm or the law is doing.

All of those things take seconds and keep you visible to a universe that has already given you their express permission to stay in touch.

9. Ask for testimonials

For some reason, asking for testimonials can cause some trepidation. In my experience, it doesn't need to be that way. You are only asking people you know are happy with your services and happy to work with you to *say* that they're happy with your services and happy to work with you.

In the majority of cases, if you have a genuine working relationship with your clients, the chances are they'll end up asking you to write the testimonial and send the draft to them for review before they sign it off.

Theoretically speaking, the reason for asking for testimonials is that they are the most powerful advertising message a prospective client will see. It is much more likely they will take notice of and react to a positive statement written by someone just like them than they would to paragraphs of expertly written copy.

The practical reason to ask is that it gives you yet another chance to get in touch (and maintain visibility) and make sure your clients continue to think of you in a positive light.

10. Let Google do the work

Though figures vary on an almost weekly basis, the general trend is that more than half of the first enquiries sent to law firms from prospective clients are made as a result of a Google search. This means you need to maintain your virtual visibility as well as your physical visibility.

Keep the search engines working for you by adding fresh content to your website and to your social media platforms. It doesn't need to be written by you (although obviously it's better if some of it is) but, across the team or across the firm, you need to keep producing different ways of refreshing the key search terms linked to your practice, terms that will respond to the searches your potential clients are most likely to make.

The proven three-step implementation model – Confidence, focus, action

So far in this chapter, we have looked at why a more intelligent (i.e. high-impact/low-cost) approach to marketing is required, why 'intelligent marketing' trumps the more traditional and more expensive marketing gestures, and at some of the most time- and cost-efficient 'intelligent marketing' activities you could make use of.

However, what we haven't looked at yet is how best to implement your preferred options. As I've already mentioned, we are going to look at the practicalities of implementing the different parts of your marketing plan (networking, speaking, writing, and researching) in more detail later in the book, but the important thing to do at this point is to get your mind-set right.

To help even the most inexperienced business developer recognise the right mind-set, at Size 10½ Boots we use a very simple three-step model: confidence, focus, action (as illustrated in Figure 1).

Figure 1: Confidence, focus, action

1. Confidence

In order to create genuine interest, you need to be confident. This doesn't need to manifest itself as cosmetic gusto or in hugely extrovert gestures (in fact, a quiet confidence is always a much more attractive proposition). It does, however, mean that you need to know exactly what you are talking about and be able to use the right anecdotes and reference points to underline that positon.

The first thing you need to be confident in is yourself. Have a think about what you do well and what you know best and try to support those thoughts with examples of where your work has been praised by a client, colleague, or contact.

Have confidence in your firm. Know your flagship clients and your best-known pieces of work. Also, have a working knowledge of your firm's various practice areas. I would never recommend you talk at length about this to further your cause during any type of conversation, but it can be good to nod sagely at the relevant point and cursorily drop in a pertinent name or past success.

Lastly, be confident in the full scope of what you and your firm offers, but more importantly, be confident in how your services really *benefit* your clients, contacts, and targets.

We have looked at how to construct a client value proposition at both firm and personal levels. I cannot stress highly enough just how pivotal this message is to the success of all of your marketing endeavours. Always remember the people you are talking to have not seen your preparatory notes, so don't suffer a crisis of confidence if you suddenly realise you've missed out a particular point. Similarly, your delivery will improve and become more natural with practice so *keep at it*. Even for the shyest amongst us, familiarity and repetition will boost confidence very quickly.

2. Focus
Yet again, we come back to the point that you only have limited time, budget, and resources for marketing and business development so you need to focus. By this stage, you should have identified your key targets whether those are:

- Totally new targets;
- Those amongst your existing client base you think are most likely to generate new work;
- Those within your professional network you think are most likely to generate referrals most frequently; or
- A mix of any or all of these groups.

Focus your attentions on the activities that will make you more visible to your chosen targets, do them well, and do them consistently. Forget about any additional activities; they are a gamble and will eat into the time and budget you have available, which will have a negative effect on the progress of your chosen strategies.

Also, focus on your chosen activities (those you have decided you are best at and actually enjoy doing). Don't get waylaid by invitations from colleagues or contacts trying to persuade you to help them out with additional initiatives.

3. Action

This is where we will borrow the slogan of a well-known American sports apparel manufacturer. Once you are confident with what you have to offer, know who you want to offer it to, and have decided how best to get your message over to that audience, you need to *just do it*.

Even if you have the best plan on paper, if you don't actually put it into action and keep it going consistently on a 'little and often' basis, it will not generate any returns. Many clients ask me if I'm willing to guarantee that, if they put what we've agreed into practice, they will win new work. Obviously, I can't do so as there are too many variables involved (demand, timing, current supply), but the guarantee I am willing to make is if you don't do any of it, you *definitely won't* generate any new work.

An understanding of your offering, an awareness of your most probable sources of work, and an appreciation of the best routes between your services and their most likely markets are all vital building blocks of a successful marketing plan; but if you are not ready, willing, and able to put them into action, your personal business development plan simply will not succeed.

Chapter 4:
How to stay visible to what you've already got

For some reason, when marketing or business development is mentioned lawyers immediately think the main objective has to be new client acquisition. I have absolutely no idea why. Whichever point of view you approach marketing from, surely it must be easier to win more work from the clients you already have? After all, these are all people or businesses that know you and trust you, people and businesses who have already made a confirmed purchasing decision to buy legal services from you in the past.

Of the three possible sources of work open to any lawyer (more work from current clients, more referrals from other professionals, gaining more new clients), by far the easiest channel to open up is your current client base. In fact, it isn't just the easiest to open up; it is also the most comfortable, given that you have already established contact. With that in mind, investing time with your current clients should arguably be your number one marketing priority. When it comes to staying visible to what you already have, your first objective must be to *keep* what you already have.

We all know that the legal market is more competitive and cut-throat than it has ever been, and this trend shows no sign of abating or reversing. Other firms are not only eyeing up your clients, they are also making active strides to take them away from you.

If you are going to grow your practice year in year out, you will need to keep your client retention rate as high as you possibly can. It is an unfortunate, but inevitable, fact that you will lose clients for a variety of reasons. But if you can develop and maintain a model that keeps the vast majority happy, you will end up keeping the vast majority of your clients. Yes, doing good work is obviously a major factor when it comes to keeping your clients happy, but it can never be considered the only factor.

Have you ever taken time out to think about what your clients value, how they like to communicate, what they consider to be an acceptable turnaround time, and how best to bill them? Have you ever thought about what really represents 'added value'? (As a steer, if that second exercise is to yield a meaningful conclusion, you will need to concentrate on deciphering and defining the 'value' part, not the 'added' part.)

What does represent real value for each client, over and above the legal advice you provide? I can't provide the answer here as I don't know your clients, but what I do know is a lazy 'one size fits all' – like a newsletter or an off-the-shelf training session – will not be the answer. And remember, when it comes to your current client base, winning more work directly from your clients should not be your sole objective. You should also be looking to deliver a level of service and create a level of visibility that will encourage your clients to generate new opportunities for you by way of personal referral.

Change your mantra from client management to client development

Thanks in no small part to the growth of CRM (client relationship management) software, 'CRM' or 'client management' have become terms the bulk of the legal profession use when they are discussing how to retain and then win more work from their current clients. However, to me, using the term 'management' suggests the only objective is retention when the focus that should be employed by any ambitious practice is actually growth. This is why my first suggestion to anyone looking to improve the way they market to their current client base is to change the term they use (and the tactics they adopt) from 'client management' to 'client development'.

To some, this may look like semantics or unnecessary pedantry, but as with all areas of marketing and business development, using the right language is absolutely essential. By making this tiny change, you are underlining exactly what you want your efforts to achieve – you don't just want to make sure your clients are looked after, you want to develop them so that:

1. They use your services more often;

2. They use more of the services your practice offers; and

3. They start to use the services offered by the other practice areas within your firm.

A client relationship is an active organism and you need to keep doing things to nurture that organism if it is going to continue to develop. It is all too easy to consider management as little more than the maintenance of the current situation, nothing more than keeping things going as they are.

The other strength of adopting development as your mantra is that it gives you a definite start (where your relationship is) and a definite end (where you want your relationship to be/ where you would like the fee levels associated with each relationship to be), which in turn allows you to put a contact plan together that will help you successfully deliver both your visibility and financial objectives.

Ten client development strategies that really work

When it comes to your contact plan, you need to make sure things stay fresh, which means you will need to vary the type of contact you have with your clients. You will also need to make sure the contact you have seems natural rather than forced and, to make sure your invitations to meet up continue to receive a positive response, that each contact delivers some value for the client.

Here are some proven contact strategies you can make use of:

1. Just stay visible

Given both the title and the key theme of this book, it is probably no surprise that this heads the list. However, it is astonishing how many law firms still treat their clients as matters in isolation rather than as a going concern.

If you are going to read no further down this list, then make sure you digest and act on this point. Once you conclude a matter, don't drop off the radar: add the client to your mailing list (making sure, of course, they only receive practical and relevant content); send them a Christmas card; make them aware of seminars or workshops that may be of interest.

I always remember talking to an old contact from my Lloyd's of London days who told me he'd used a well-known Surrey firm when he moved house. After he'd moved he heard nothing from them ever again, which ended up costing the firm. As an experienced and savvy professional, the client realised not only would he and his wife have to make new wills, but also that he needed more long-term help re-appropriating his capital and assets so he could meet his children's upcoming university fees. That work could have gone to the same firm he had previously used, but having disappeared after the final bill for the conveyancing was issued, the firm didn't win this work. Instead, it went to their competitors.

More worryingly for the firm that undertook the conveyancing, my contact was also in a senior position in the procurement chain in a large Japanese insurance company who had a need for regular private client support for their executives. Predictably, the firm never saw any of that work either.

2. Phone vs. email

Email is a tempting offer. It's quick and it makes it so much easier to rattle through your 'to-do' list when it feels time is against you. Conversely, it is a massively impersonal medium and, although it's the perfect means with which to deliver correspondence quickly and efficiently, it goes against one of the most important pillars in a client/lawyer relationship: bespoke advice delivered in person by a professional.

Wherever possible, try to give an answer by telephone. From a service point of view it maintains that all-important personal contact. It also underlines the fact you genuinely care about delivering your advice in a way that allows additional questions to be asked there and then so the client attains the highest level of value from your input. From a more mercenary point of view, it is amazing how much more work more contact and more conversation creates.

3. Chewing the fat

Far too many lawyers still think their clients are too busy to meet up for a chat and that any request to catch up in person is nothing short of an imposition. Clients have a very different perspective. They want the opportunity to 'chew the fat' from time to time. And this is not a phrase chosen at random because it sounds good; it has been taken verbatim from a number of client services reviews we have undertaken. It is also a phrase that is nearly always suffixed with 'and if they did, they'd get more work'.

As long as your contact is spaced out throughout the year, your clients will welcome the chance to sit down and talk about their life, their universe, and everything in between. Because of your legal training and your wider client experience, you can offer a very different perspective on pretty much any personal or commercial situation they might be experiencing, and it is this difference in approach that delivers real value for the client.

4. Walking the floor

As an extension to simply sitting down and chewing the fat, you can go one stage further and ask to be walked around some-one's business premises. Remember, these people will have given blood, sweat, and tears to get their businesses up and running, and therefore the current operation will be a source of enormous pride to them. Having the opportunity to show someone around will never be refused.

During the tour, ask questions about specific parts of the production line, ask about future plans, ask about expansion plans and possible diversifications. You have a captive audience who will welcome the opportunity to answer all of these questions and every answer could provide a chance for more work or a reason to stay in touch (and stay visible) long into the future.

Moreover, although walking the floor could possibly be construed as a commercial-only strategy, it also works for private client lawyers. All businesses will have staff, and it may be possible to strike a deal by which you can offer, for example, wills to those members of staff. If that isn't a possibility, then all of the business owners and senior managers will have personal networks made up of people they could refer you to.

5. Five minutes

I'm going to make the assumption that you are more than willing to give any client five minutes on the phone without charging, if they need a quick answer to a quick question. The only thing is, do your clients actually know that option is available to them?

Make sure your clients know you are ready, willing, and able to take the odd question as and when they arise. Not only will this engender a massive amount of goodwill (tying you in even closer to your clients and making it more likely they'll refer you on to contacts, family, and friends), it also makes it almost impossible for the client to turn elsewhere should the answer you give them require additional legal support, which means those five minutes are more than likely to become a direct work generator.

6. Becoming a virtual director

This is the perfect way to formalise the idea of walking the floor. Offer to sit in on your clients' board meetings and be prepared to offer a legal perspective on the key issues. Again, your outlook will be slightly different and will add another dimension to discussions, whether that added dimension is a more effective way of achieving a desired outcome or a necessary note of caution should the objective be less practical.

You don't need to go to every meeting – maybe one or two a year – but as long as you are willing to participate then your attendance gives you the perfect opportunity both to underline your understanding of the business (or their charity or educational facility if those are the organisations relevant to your practice) and your technical skills, and get close to key stakeholders you may not ordinarily have access to at the same time.

For a private client lawyer, this approach works just as well when it comes to the organising committees of a local association or club or to the board of governors at a local school. All of these entities are made up of people who could either use you or refer you to someone they know may need advice.

7. Trend, angle, hook

When you spend time with your clients, you will build up a working knowledge of their business or organisation and their market. You can use that understanding to help you pick up pieces of useful information and use them as a way to maintain contact and visibility. Again, taking a more mercenary standpoint, each could also be a route to a new piece of work.

The best model I have found to make the most effective use of industry information is 'trend, angle, hook'. Once you recognise the trends in a particular market, you can use your understanding of your clients' businesses to see how a particular piece of information could be of use to your client (whether it is an opportunity or a threat); this is your angle.

You then present the piece of information alongside the angle and ask if they'd like to discuss the potential ramifications; this is your hook. Again, it is a strategy that has to be used sparingly and only when the information at hand is directly relevant to your client. Getting in touch and putting a hook forward every other week will soon become transparent and irritating.

8. Client service reviews

I have already mentioned a few of the gems we at Size 10 ½ Boots have uncovered as a result of undertaking client service review programmes for our clients. Although the feedback was given on the performance of particular fee earners from particular firms for particular clients, I trust you can see that many of the comments made are much more widely applicable.

Client service reviews are an essential component of any client development model. Firstly, if you are promoting the fact that you view the need to provide your clients with the highest level of service as your main priority, your boast will not be credible unless you are employing some sort of personal feedback mechanism.

Secondly, if a handful of your clients are asking for the same thing or making the same points or criticisms regarding specific aspects of your service delivery, the chances are that many other existing and prospective clients would say the same thing given half a chance. This means there are things that either need to be promoted (if you are doing them) or adopted (if you are not).

Again, I have never come across a situation where the request for time to provide this level of feedback has been taken as an imposition. Clients recognise it is in their interests to provide this feedback because they will end up receiving a better, more comprehensive, and more rounded service as a result of it.

With regards to the delivery of client service interviews, there are two ways to approach them. One way is to ask either your managing partner, or a partner who is not involved in the day-to-day management of the client, to conduct the interviews so there is a degree of impartiality. However, the best results are achieved when a third party undertakes the review because they are totally independent and the subject will feel more at ease giving completely open feedback. If you do go down the third party route, you will also receive a positive PR bump because the client will see you care enough about your relationship to invest in sending someone to interview them on your behalf.

9. Recognise the client as a person first and client second

Every client is an individual and therefore has an individual set of likes, dislikes, and interests. Spending time together means you will find out what many of those things are. Once you know what each of your clients likes to do, you can use that information to design a client contact plan that plays directly to their likes and avoids their dislikes.

Don't invite a non-golfer to a golf day or a football fan to a rugby match. Similarly, don't ask someone who prefers a quick coffee (in a particular coffee house) to go for a long leisurely lunch, or someone who prefers breakfast so they can get on with their day for a pint or a glass of wine after work.

Hanging your invitations on personal preferences is massively flattering to clients more used to being invited to things for the sake of being invited. This more tailored approach will mark you out from the run of the mill professionals in your market. It will also increase the chances of your invitees responding positively to your invitations, which in turn will increase your face time with them and the likelihood the resultant conversations will be more open and more productive.

10. FFH (football, families, holidays)

As your relationships develop, they should take a more social and personal shape. Make a note (mentally or physically) of the things your clients have going on outside of work. My old director at Lloyds always told me that if you knew which team they supported (and again, like 'coffee', 'football' is a catch-all), about their family circumstances, and about their holidays, you would always have something to talk about.

On the surface, this relates more to the time you spend with clients and giving you ammunition you can use to keep the small talk going that will fill in the gaps between the meatier topics. However, under the surface, it is active business development gold.

One patent attorney we work with uses the marquee golf tournaments to stay visible to his key contacts in the US, all of whom play golf. They wind each other up via text during a tournament, arguing about the relative merits of the Americans and Europeans involved. As a result, planning a full diary for the next trip to the US is easy as it only needs another text message.

Similarly, one head of a barristers' chambers we worked with picked up on a comment made by an instructing solicitor about the fact they were about to be out of the office for a fortnight. He asked where she was going and the solicitor told him she was off to the north coast of Mallorca. Not only had the barrister been there, but he also still had the guidebook he used so he walked it round to the solicitor's offices and delivered it personally. Unsurprisingly, this simple gesture resulted in an increase in instructions upon the solicitor's return.

How to grow your existing client relationships
When it comes to growing your client relationships there are two approaches you can employ:

1. Look at your own practice – How can you win more work from your clients?

2. Look at the rest of your firm's client base – Which of the clients who use any of the other practice areas offered by your firm should also be using you?

Depending on your practice area and how confident you are when it comes to BD, you may either wish to choose one of these to start with or a mixture of both. If you are going to choose one, I would recommend number one as, again, it's easier and more comfortable and therefore more likely to work, which will give you more confidence to move on to number two in the future.

Wherever you choose to start, you need to put a simple, easy-to-follow plan together. There is a plethora of client development templates readily available at the end of any Google search, but these tend to have been developed for corporate sales efforts so they can be a little over-complicated. Given that you have other responsibilities, I would (as always) suggest you keep things as simple as possible. In this case, simplicity falls into a very straightforward four-step plan:

1. Objective – What is your objective for that particular client? To keep them? To grow their spend? Or to sell them other services?

2. Goals – Under that main objective, what are your goals? How much do you plan to grow their spend? Which other services do you plan to sell them? Which other areas of the business do you want as clients? Who else within their organisation (or among their family/friends if you are a private client lawyer) do you want as clients? Or it may be you want them to do something for you, invite you to join one of their trade associations or a member-only organisation they belong to, or introduce you to other targets within your chosen markets.

3. Strategies – This part houses your tactics. How are you going to achieve your goals? How, when, and where will you see them? What will you invite them to? What will you offer as added value, and how/when/where will you deliver that additional value? What do you need to do to meet the other people you want to know in that business, organisation, or family?

4. Measures – These are the targets you need to hit to make sure your strategies are on course for success. It may be you want to see people once a quarter or send them one 'saw this and thought of you' per month. It may be you want to speak to them once a month on the telephone.

The mistake too many lawyers make is to focus these measures on the financial – you need to achieve £x in fees per year

– but the truth is meaningful, long-term success is based on performance indicators rather than financial indicators. In plain English, that means doing stuff, not raising bills. If you see your client consistently and make sure you talk about things other than work so your personal relationship develops, the bills will take care of themselves.

Implementing a plan for your existing clients

If you follow the steps above, you will have the skeleton of a client development plan you can put into action immediately. Without wanting to sound glib, it is then solely down to you. You need to make sure the tactics you've set are delivered on time and in the right frequency, and that you meet the measurements you've set yourself.

The good news is that while you can only see people one at a time (as least if you are going to have the type of meaningful conversations that will deepen relationships and ultimately generate work) the in-betweeny-joiny-up stuff required to keep the wheels spinning – activities like providing industry intelligence, 'saw this and thought of you' type emails, making sure people are reminded the five-minute quick question offer is there for them – can be replicated and/or automated to lighten the load.

Implementing a plan for your firm's existing clients

Although your one-page plan will give you the necessary guidelines for each client target (what you need to do, how you need to do it, and by when) and the ultimate responsibility for making it work will stay with you, this is where you can share the load amongst your colleagues and use that collegiate approach to spur each other on. The two case studies that follow are examples of successful cross-selling/internal collaboration at work.

Buddying up for mutual benefit

There is an old sales cliché that says: 'people buy from people they like and people who are like them'. This is why, when helping a client to look at new ways to cross-sell services, we came up with the suggestion that the most likely route to a new opportunity would be to choose a colleague to introduce who is similar in personality and approach to the fee earner who is currently the target's key point of contact.

We examined each target client's current spend (in terms of practice area rather than volume) and then worked out a matrix showing which services they took and which they should be taking. From there, we highlighted the gaps and identified a lawyer that complemented the lead fee earner in terms of style. The lead fee earner then set up a very informal meeting and took along their 'buddy', not to sell but just to be introduced. This is the crucial part: *there was no pitch*. Their objective was to mention in passing what they did and then just to concentrate on clicking with the client.

Over a six-month period and an initial universe of 10 targets, nine of the clients introduced to additional fee earners made further enquiries and, of those, four progressed the replies they received to those enquiries to an instruction.

Internal JVs

While law firms have traditionally been very good at partnering up with other professionals and third-party organisations when it comes to putting on seminars, for some reason internal cooperation between departments is rare.

Having adopted more of a sector-based approach (something we'll look at in more detail in Mini-masterclass 1), we helped our client to build a series of cross-departmental sector teams that were made up of fee earners from all of the relevant practice areas. One of their key initiatives was to design a workshop that covered all of the potential legal issues a client in that sector could face, all of which were presented by the fee earner from the practice areas involved.

To ensure the firm generated the highest level of value and return for the time they'd put into the preparation of the workshop, it was then rolled out in three ways:

1. To small, specifically chosen groups of clients who used one or, at most, two practice areas, but should have been using several more. Keeping the groups small ensured a higher level of engagement and interaction;

2. To larger audiences made up of existing and lapsed clients, prospects, and other influencers and professionals linked to the sector in question; and

3. As a third stage, the session was also offered to the firm's larger clients in the sector as an onsite training package.

As a by-product, the content was also turned into a series of e-shots and downloads that extended the team's reach into their sector further still.

The (almost immediate) result of this approach was the clients invited to the smaller groups started to take up the other services the firm had showcased. The larger, more general audience also generated enquiries which have since been followed up on and have opened up new opportunities. Meanwhile, the in-house training has been very well received. It has also created new opportunities for other parts of the firm, as well as introductions to other companies and contacts in their sector that the clients who received the training thought would also benefit from the session.

Chapter 5:
Don't just stay visible to clients, stay visible to referrers

In the last chapter, we looked at how to look after your clients. I stand by my claim that this should always be your number one marketing priority. The only trouble is, if you are investing all of your time in client development (not management), who is taking care of your referrers?

I think it is still fair to say referrers are probably the single most productive source of new business opportunities for law firms of any size and in any sector. In spite of this, the majority of fee earners still rely on what is in their heads to manage these vital relationships, and they depend on nothing more scientific than instinct to measure the success of each relationship, and the return it generates.

I can only assume that it is the lack of obviousness and immediacy that pushes referral relationship management out of your eye-line. With new business (whether new matters are coming from existing clients or from new targets), it's all very easy to track. You get the call saying you've got the job, you open the file, everyone can see the result, and you get a pat on the back. With referrers, it works the opposite way. You don't notice they've gone (most likely to one of your competitors) until the flow of work you took for granted stops.

I'd actually go further to try to explain the impact that not taking care of referrers more actively will have on your practice. I am confident enough to say in print – as I have to many managing partners and heads of department I have worked with – that if your firm was to stop all of its advertising and sponsorship tomorrow, you'd notice a minimal difference to the level of new enquiries your firm generates. However, if you were to discontinue all of your contact with your key referrers, the effect on your pipeline would be severe and immediate.

Some of the less marketing-friendly lawyers we've worked with have told us they can't market their practices because they are either distress purchases (litigation, family) or part of a chain that's already been established before they're invited to join (corporate). The only trouble is, to me at least, this just seems to be a way of avoiding business development, rather than a valid reason not to do it, particularly as the majority of the nay-sayers have invested little in terms of establishing a process that would maintain, maximise, and expand their referrer network.

This is a dangerous strategy. The immediate and obvious effect of not being organised is that your visibility will dip in key areas and this will mean you miss out on a few matters here and there. The real danger, however, is that your competitors – all of whom covet your professional relationships as much as they covet your client relationships – will have an opportunity to step in. If you are not making regular contact, if you're not making sure work is flowing back and forth and generally making your relationship worthwhile for both sides, then you run the risk of creating a space that will be filled quickly and hungrily by your competitors.

Why referrers are as valuable as clients

First off, let's try to define the term 'referrer'. To my mind, it breaks down into three core groups:

1. Professionals – This is the most traditional definition. It usually means accountants or bankers, but there are other professions that are one-step removed from you that can offer even more help to particular practice areas, e.g. VCs and business angels for IP/IT and corporate lawyers; IFAs and wealth managers for private client lawyers; commercial agents, surveyors, architects, and developers for commercial property lawyers; wedding planners for family lawyers; etc.

2. Industry figures – Your sector is served by a number of different professionals, all of whom have active networks (made up of prospective clients) around them. These include senior members of trade associations, journalists, event organisers, consultants, and 'fixers'.

3. Key influencers – Although this is admittedly the most amorphous group, if your sector or practice is based on a particular geography, it could be the most important. In every area there is a small band of movers and shakers who know everyone and, more importantly, what everyone's up to. These people are often invaluable introducers if not direct referrers of work.

While all of these groups may look different, the truth is they have one very significant thing in common: they all know a raft of people who could/should/would become your clients. By taking the time and making the effort to get to know them and, wherever possible, to add as much value as possible, your efforts will pay off in terms of referrals and introductions.

Better still, they will do your selling for you. By the time you meet the client, they will already have a positive view of you because your name will have been put forward by someone they trust and have an existing relationship with. This means they will already accept you have the required technical skills so, at the very worst, all you will need to do is prove that you have a style and personality that they would feel comfortable working with.

Sometimes, it is this more personal aspect that causes nervousness for lawyers. This shouldn't be the case. In the next section, we will move on to how to build an effective referrer network. Part of that process will be to choose the people you want to work with and exchange work with and some of that will come down to intangibles like 'click', 'fit', or 'like-mindedness'. That means that you will ultimately gravitate toward people who are similar to you, and if those professionals have already been accepted by the client being referred to you, the chances are that client will warm to you too.

How do you build a referrer relationship model that really works?

It may not be what you want to hear, but if you are to effectively manage your professional network, you need to adopt a more systemised approach that will:

- Make sure you see everyone;
- Make sure you know which referrers actually generate work;
- Make sure you know where additional referral opportunities lie outside your current network; and
- Make sure those who you do exchange referrals with feel valued.

Step 1: Identification

The first step is to list your key contacts. Have you ever taken time out to think about who you give work to most frequently? Or, more importantly, about who gives you work most frequently? Because of the way human beings are wired up, it's often the case that you associate the highest levels of success with those you like most, but this is not always the case. All too often, it is easy for a lawyer to spend the bulk of their time with the people they get on with best, misguidedly assuming they're spending their marketing time efficiently. The only trouble is, some of the contacts that do regularly introduce new opportunities may only be seen sporadically (if at all), and if this is the case then your marketing efforts will never yield the results they should.

You need to be disciplined and look at all of your professional relationships clinically. Make a list of the professionals you are in regular or even semi-regular contact with. Then think about the last 12 months. Which have given you work/

introductions and which have you given work/introductions to? Don't let overcomplicating this step delay you; if you can't run off a report from your case management system, then a good old fashioned 'five bar gate' approach is more than sufficient for this exercise.

One question we are often asked at this stage is: 'What about the ones I know could be good, but haven't come good yet?' It's a good question. The answer is you need to make a judgement call.

If you are confident:

- The person you are pursuing is well known;
- They tend to crop up more often than not at the good events;
- They are obviously known at those events; and
- They will come good,

then keep going with them.

The only addendum I'd suggest is to give yourself a cut-off date. If tangible progress has not been made (and tangible progress doesn't necessarily mean a concrete referral; it could just as well be an introduction or a firm promise that you will get the legal work when one of their prospects drops) within 12 months, maybe it is time to move on.

What this stage is meant to catch are the perennial lunchers/sports ticket takers/invitation for a pint accepters who have talked a good game (and have used up a significant portion of your marketing time and budget) over a period of time and delivered absolutely nothing. When you sit down and have a proper think, I can assure you these people will identify themselves. Of course, identification doesn't mean total exclusion. You can still maintain a veneer of interest by inviting them to your firm's social events and seminars and workshops, and you will undoubtedly see them regularly at other firms' events and at networking events.

Step 2: Segmentation

Now that you have your core list, you need to order them according to return. Those who deliver the most should get the most investment (in terms of time, frequency, and expense), the second group slightly less, and those who you think may offer long-term opportunity but where there's currently no real relationship require a different approach again.

When we looked at identifying your key professional relationships, I asked you to be clinical. When it comes to segmenting that list into your primary and secondary referrers, you need to go one step beyond – you need to be brutal.

However buoyant your practice may be, there's only so much work you can send back the other way, so try to be realistic in terms of numbers. Keeping a manageable group (10–12) happy is so much better than trying to re-enact that famous trick with the loaves and fishes.

Step 3: Diarise

Now you have your contacts and have ordered those contacts in terms of how often you need to see them. The next stage is to diarise that contact so that: a) it happens; and b) you know it has happened. While this may seem like a superfluous step, if you are anything like me, then when you suddenly think of someone you need to see your involuntary reaction will be that you 'only saw them the other week'. The only problem is, when you look back through your diary, it could be the wrong side of six months since you actually did see them.

Diarising takes away the doubt and takes responsibility for your contact campaign out of the hands of your memory and onto paper. Again, we're not talking about extensive memoranda; I'm suggesting the simplest possible aide memoir. The template in Figure 1 is the one we use at Size 10 ½ Boots, and you can either take the easy approach (putting a cross in the box) or the more complicated one (adding the type of contact you'll be making). Either way, it takes seconds to keep up to date, but we know from experience those few seconds more than deliver

	Jan	Feb	Mar	Apr	May	Jun	Jul	Aug	Sep	Oct	Nov	Dec
PR1*	Lunch	Coffee	Coffee	Awards dinner	Lunch		Coffee	Golf	Rugby	Coffee		Lunch
PR2	Round table	Coffee				Lunch	Coffee		Rugby		Curry	
PR3	Lunch	Football		Coffee	Drinks		Coffee	Team event		Coffee		
PR4	Coffee			Awards dinner					Drinks	Football		Drinks
PR5		Lunch			Curry				Drinks			Coffee
SR1+	×		×	×		×			×			×
SR2			×					×		×		
SR3		×					×				×	
SR4		×				×					×	
SR5	×			×	×				×			
SR6				×				×				×

Key:
*PR: Primary referrer
+SR: Secondary referrer

Figure 1: Template to help you diarise your contacts[1]

69

in terms of keeping you visible and making sure you are front of mind when opportunities for work to be referred to you arise.

Step 4: Make all future marketing more effective

Aside from making you more effective and more visible, there is another benefit associated with a more structured approach to referrer relationship management. When it comes to explaining what a benefit is, I always describe it as something that does one, two, or three of three things:

1. It'll save you time;

2. It'll save you money; and/or

3. It'll save you hassle.

Adopting a more structured approach to managing your professional relationships is no different. When you manage it properly, your network will make sure you are receiving a steady flow of new work. By extension, this means you will save the time you would otherwise have had to invest in finding new business opportunities. That includes:

- The time you would need to spend going to less effectual networking events (and again if, like me, you dislike formal networking, it gives you a reason to get out of it – what boss would make you keep on with something if you had found something more productive and more cost-effective to replace it?); and

- The time (and hassle) you would otherwise expend on constantly trying to invent new marketing messages and methods (time you could better use for billable client work).

However, it also means you will spend less on marketing. One coffee with a proven referrer will cost £5 (£7 with a cake), but it will deliver more than designing, printing, and mailing a new brochure. Add to this that it will take a lot less time and effort than drafting the brochure and getting six partners to agree the copy, colours, and mailing list!

How do you grow your professional network?
For ease of reference, I'm going to split this into two parts:

1. Getting started at the beginning of your (marketing) career; and

2. Improving your professional network as your career progresses.

Once established, your objective becomes cementing and deepening your relationships so that you are not only consistently visible, but also that you are the contact most associated with adding value. The following case studies illustrate some options you could use to underline that value and become more visible at the same time.

External JVs

It will come as no surprise to you, but many of the firms we work with already have an established programme of joint seminars and workshops. The benefit for the attendee is they leave with a more rounded understanding of a particular topic, which should theoretically have a positive effect on the take-up for places.

There are also huge practical benefits for the two firms involved. Running a seminar or event with an accountant, property agent, IFA, or wealth manager gives you the opportunity to tap in to the other party's client base, which should increase attendance and the likelihood that attendance will introduce you to someone new. It also allows you to share the cost (and time) of planning, promoting, and running an event, not to mention following-up with the attendees.

However, the hidden benefit is that it also gives those organising the event a reason to spend more time together and get to know each other much better and this, as long as it is followed up and the two fee earners stay in touch, is often the way a joint marketing venture delivers a truly long-term return.

Round tables (covering the educational and the social)

One of the teams we work with at a mid-tier firm decided they placed the highest value on three of their relationships. As a result, it was agreed their BD priority had to be to strengthen and grow them.

On top of the regular, individual 'coffee' contact and making sure the referrers were invited to the main industry events throughout the year, the team decided they were going to host a series of informal 'round tables' each quarter. The agenda was simple: to discuss the key issues affecting their sector. They would provide a legal perspective; the contacts would provide their perspective; and both teams would leave with a better understanding of the part both played within the purchasing process, insight that could be utilised to improve the quality of service both sides provided for their respective clients.

However, rather than just ticking the educational box (for which they also offered CPD points as an extra incentive), they made sure the session was started mid-morning. This meant they could provide a sandwich lunch afterwards that allowed them to interact more socially and start conversations that could be followed up with an invite to meet up one-on-one.

As a result of these events, the team has seen an upturn in the number of referrals they receive from all three of the referrers they picked. They have also gone some way to safeguard their future referrals by increasing the links between members of both teams at all levels, rather than just relying on the links at the senior end.

Make it fun

Why do meetings have to be in work and about work all of the time? If we get on with people, why can't we meet up and do things we like? These are questions one of our clients asked when we were looking at ways of strengthening their professional relationships.

Unsurprisingly, the answer to both questions was that there was no reason at all.

As a result, we looked at the make-up of the firm's teams and the corresponding teams in their referrer organisations and drew up a social calendar of things the respective teams working together would actually enjoy doing. The list was different from practice area to practice area, but included mountain biking, beer tasting, cocktail making, cake decorating, table football, and pool. The result was that the firm established wider and stronger links with their key referrers, and the improved links not only generated more work but also a more effective way of working together, which was appreciated and commented upon by their mutual clients.

How do you convert your relationships into work?

If you have followed the steps above, you now have a list of the contacts you need to stay visible to and a diary of events that will keep you visible. Now, we need to look at the end result: turning that visibility into billable work.

In the majority of cases, just being in touch – or at least front of mind – is enough. If you have built up a genuine relationship, you will become the first port of call when your key referrers come across a piece of work that requires your particular set of skills. This means that horrible things like 'selling', 'pitching', and 'closing' can become a thing of the past. As long as you choose the right contacts and take care of your relationships properly, consistently, and systematically, they should produce results with very little input.

However, at the start of a relationship there may be a need to find a catalyst to grease the wheels and get you started. If you're finding that is the case with some of your contacts, here are five ideas you could use:

1. Ask!

That's often all it takes: a simple (well-timed) question. But even though things are ticking along nicely on the social front, all too many professionals are afraid to ask for that first opportunity.

Obviously, I wouldn't suggest a pushy 'Give me a job' approach, but a softer suggestion like 'We've known each other a while and I'd really like an opportunity to work together… ' or 'Do you think we're at a point where you would be comfortable to send some work to me… ' is more than permissible.

The first thing to note is you will be surprised how many times this type of question will be answered positively. It's easy for people to: a) forget why you're meeting up because they enjoy your company; and b) get set in their ways, referring work to particular individuals out of habit rather than desire. The fact you have asked will be flattering and will start them thinking: 'Hang on, I like them, they seem good at their job, and maybe it is time we moved things forward.'

Secondly, if they say no, then they're more than likely to follow that with the reason why. Don't worry about this. If you've spent time together and they are happy to accept your invitations, it will not be personal. It is more likely to be to do with long-standing reciprocal relationships, to a perceived hole in your skill set, or a little bit of caution when it comes to nudging the status quo. All of these can be addressed and overturned over time (not there and then; you're not a double glazing tele-salesperson!).

One response I've seen work well in several contexts is to leave the conversation there, but to ask if you could assume the positon of 'first substitute', i.e. if their regular referee in your field is busy or lets them down, would they be happy bringing you off the bench as their first substitute. Not only is this unthreatening, it also reinforces the fact you are genuinely interested in working together, but won't be irritatingly pushy about it.

2. Send work the other way

Just as one of the easiest ways to get clients to endorse you on LinkedIn is to endorse them, one of the easiest ways to open up a two-way exchange of referrals is to take the lead and offer your contact the first referral. Reciprocity is a wonderful thing and there are very few people who will not send something back the other way.

3. Make introductions

Ignoring the overwhelming urge to begin with some nonsense about every journey beginning with a single step, I am going to start by saying that (in my experience at least) every business relationship starts with a conversation.

If you can bring a particular client into a conversation – 'I was just thinking, I bet you'd get on really well with [add client name here]. Would you like me to set up a coffee/beer/lunch?' – it will allow you to bring your relationship onto the next footing quickly and effectively while leaving the door open for your contact to respond in kind.

You can also take this one step further by asking a contact if they'd be amenable to meeting up to go through a shortlist of six clients each, clients you both think the other could work with. From there, you'll probably whittle the list down to a manageable two or three and can start making the arrangements to introduce each other to your respective final shortlists.

4. Hypothesise

I am neither a psychologist nor a Jedi Knight, but there are certain ways you can bring a conversation round to where you want it to be. One of those ways is to hypothesise.

Try to find reasons to talk about 'the best of all possible worlds'. Ask your contact, if you were to work together, how would they like to be kept in the loop. Ask what type of legal advisor, ideally, do they think their different clients would work best with, or would like to work with. Ask them how, if you did get that first chance to do some work for their clients, you could add more value to the relationship.

Each answer will allow you to nod sagely and give an example as to how you have done exactly that in the past. This positive reinforcement will allow you to start peeling away any lingering doubts that you are the right person for them to refer their clients to. More subliminally, it gets them to actually picture what it would be like to work with you, which will help them to dispel those doubts from their own minds.

If all this sounds like mumbo-jumbo, let me stress I am pragmatic to the point of cynicism and I certainly wouldn't have embarrassed myself by including it if I hadn't seen it work.

5. Make more of your experience

'I was only saying to George Clooney the other day that I didn't like to name-drop.... '.

There are few things less attractive than the 'enough about me, let's talk about me' school of self-promotion; however, your past experience can be used intelligently and selectively to very good effect.

As with the previous point, less is most definitely more. When something relevant comes up in the conversation, give a quick nod of acknowledgement and drop in one line demonstrating how you successfully tackled a similar issue in the past, then move the conversation back to your contact with a 'but you were saying... '.

Again, you are, without flexing your ego or own self-importance, starting to peel away any doubts your contact might have that you are the right person to receive the referral, should the issue you are discussing get that far.

References
1. By the way, if you would like a fully working excel sheet housing this tool, just drop me an email at douglas@tenandahalf.co.uk and I'll be more than happy to send it over.

Chapter 6:
How do you create the visibility that wins new clients?

As I said in an earlier chapter, when marketing or business development is mentioned in a legal context, the tendency is to think about new client acquisition. While bringing in new clients is both a noble and necessary objective, it is also the most difficult result to achieve marketing-wise. But I stress it is *difficult*, not impossible.

There are three key reasons why new client acquisition is difficult:

1. Businesses and people already have lawyers and are happy with them;

2. Too many people (not least those selling legal services) view the purchase of legal services as a 'distress purchase' and will seek referrals from those they trust only when the need arises; and

3. Lawyers and firms just aren't as visible to their potential targets as they should be.

However, the truth is that few firms will be able to sustain any level of growth if they do not bring in new clients, so some thought must be given to how they can successfully do so. Key points to bear in mind when devising a new client strategy are illustrated in Figure 1 and explored in more detail in this chapter.

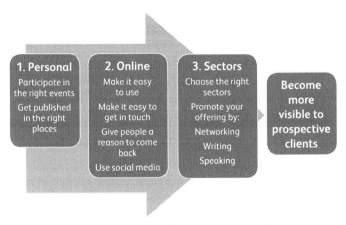

Figure 1: Your route to greater visibility with prospective clients

Make sure your firm is visible to potential new clients

This is probably stating the obvious, but your firm's overall visibility must be your first priority. If we go back to the idea of creating brand cameos (an identikit of the properties, demographics, and behaviours you're looking for in your ideal client), you will know who you want as new clients, and what are the most likely ways to get your name in front of those targets. Use that intelligence and start to take advantage of those opportunities to boost your visibility. The more people who know who you are, what you do, and how your services will benefit them, the more likely you are to generate new enquiries.

Similarly, if you are present at the right events and you are actively participating in those events, starting conversations, and following up properly, you will find those new conversations will – over time – generate new enquiries.

All of this can be cemented by press coverage (not advertising slots). If you invest in building relationships with journalists at the right publications – which may be local or trade titles depending on the location and focus of your practice – they will come to you for comment and for editorial. If your targets repeatedly see you featured in the publications they read, you will soon be recognised as an expert in your field, and this thought leadership will generate new enquiries.

Some lawyers are not comfortable with the idea of cosying up to journalists, but I cannot stress just how short sighted this is. All you need to do is invite them to your marketing events (social and educational) and make sure you spend five minutes with them to have a cup of tea, coffee, or something more exciting if they accept.

You can also meet up occasionally for a coffee to discuss what's going on in your city, region, or sector. Journalists are likely to be 'general practitioners' who will understand their subjects, but will not have the legal perspective you will be able to provide on the issues that affect their readers. They will not rebuff the offer of gaining that perspective; they will encourage and appreciate it.

Get your web presence right

Depending on which statistics you read and which week you read them in, it is generally accepted that somewhere around 60 per cent of all of the new enquiries received by law firms come in via the web. This means that your online presence is now the primary source of new client enquiries.

Obviously, these figures are skewed by the volume of enquiries generated by the more consumer-led practice areas – predominantly property, matrimonial, and will writing – but that doesn't mean the figures are not indicative of a wider trend that is driving the way law firms generate new clients.

If you ignore the continued devolvement of your web presence, you risk losing out to those of your competitors who are investing in making sure they turn up on top of the search results and that, when customers click through to their website or LinkedIn page, they're impressed by what they see.

Here is a checklist you can use to make sure you get the best return from the internet:

1. **Your website** – Does your website represent you in the right light? Does it make you look dynamic and contemporary,

or is it a bit dated? Most of all, is it smart phone responsive? As the majority of people now browse on their phones or tablets rather than their desktops, this is an increasingly important consideration, particularly for the more private client focused services. I know putting a new website together is a painfully time- and cost-consuming process, but remember it is your window to the world. If it is totally outdated, cluttered, and lacking the design impact of your competitors' sites, you may lose potential clients at the first touch point.

2. **Navigation** – Is it easy for visitors to get around your website and find out everything they need to? Again, if it is tricky or confusing, first time visitors will leave quickly… never to return! Keep it easy, keep it logical, and look at the functionality you like on the websites you use for ideas.

3. **Links** – Two things to consider here:

   o Do all of your links (to LinkedIn, Twitter, email, or microsites) work? It's easy to miss and can be off-putting to potential clients or professional contacts. After all, you are being employed for your attention to detail (amongst other things) so you need to get even the smallest details right; and

   o Do you have links to relevant third parties (clients, trade associations, sites relevant to your sectors, referrers, and partners)? All of these will have a beneficial effect on your search engine rankings.

4. **Content** – When it comes to your website, it is great if people find it, but it's better if they keep coming back. To achieve that, you need to make your site 'sticky' (e-marketing speak for giving people a reason to keep coming back). One way to do that is to keep adding content. This can be through a regular blog, by adding downloads, posting articles, adding hints and help on how to avoid/ solve certain situations; it could be by adding relevant

news from your local area or chosen sectors. It could be a bit of everything. It doesn't really matter which way you choose to go, but it does matter that the content is practical, relevant, readable, and continually updated. Continually updating your content will also have a beneficial effect on your search engine rankings. Google, in particular, reacts very well to new content and, as that's the engine almost everyone uses, it pays to play to its preferences.

5. **Social media** – Once you have fresh content coming through, use it. I am making the assumption you have a LinkedIn profile; you may even have a Twitter feed. These will only work for you visibility-wise if they are dynamic, so post and promote your content via these platforms. Every time you post/update/tweet you are reminding people you are there and, when it comes to building visibility, these light reminders are the bricks.

6. **Downloads** – We touched upon downloads under content, but one of the things you can do to make them work harder for you is to house them behind a simple registration screen. Ask people for their name and email address (no more, it puts people off) in order to unlock your advice. Once people volunteer that information, it becomes your property. You can add all of those contacts to your marketing database so you can continue to stay visible to them.

7. **Calls to action** – Every marketing mechanism needs a call to action. You need to tell people what to do next, and make it easy for them to do it. Clear and concise contact information (preferably hyperlinked to the right email address and/or phone number) is essential. And keeping all of these links up to date is also essential. Again, you are hardly underlining your incomparable attention to detail if your prospect calls the firm to be told that the person they are looking for left in 2009. You also need to offer prospects a reason to get in touch. It may be a special report

that provides more information on a particular subject; it may be a practical checklist or audit template that allows them to assess the potential risk in a situation; or it may be that old favourite, the free initial consultation. Whatever you choose, make it obvious and make it easy.

Adopting a sector strategy

Discussions around adopting a sector strategy (where you focus on specific industry groups or more defined geographies) often cause unnecessary nervousness. It's a shame because, with regard to new client acquisition, it is by far the most effective way to generate the best possible return from the limited time and resources you have available for business development.

I'd like to start by dispelling some of the myths that exist around sector strategies:

'If we employ a sector strategy we will pigeonhole ourselves'

A sector strategy is not a steel fence designed to exclude you from winning work from the areas outside of the sectors you choose; it is a way of focusing the limited time and resources you have for marketing more effectively and stacking the odds of you appearing as the credible solution to certain targets more firmly in your favour.

At no point would anyone expect you to turn down the opportunity to progress any enquiry that comes into the firm, whether that enquiry comes from a client, a contact, or from the phone or internet. Your website and literature will still show you can assist clients with corporate, commercial, property, employment, family, and private client work. However, in order to give these skills more relevance, a sector focus allows you to explain the benefits of these services in a way that clearly shows your targets how they can take full advantage of them. This will make you more credible as you progress your new client acquisition initiatives.

'If we employ a sector strategy we will lose potential opportunities'

A sector focus is not about publicly telling the world there are sources you will not accept work from; it is about using the limited time and resources you have at your disposal to win more work more effectively. It will be initiated in addition to your regular meetings with clients, contacts, and referrers – not instead of these. These meetings will still undoubtedly create introductions to potential new clients and your sector strategy won't stop you progressing these.

During the course of your sector marketing, you will also impress contacts sufficiently for them to refer you on to members of their networks who may not be members of the chosen sectors and, again, a sector strategy does not stop you progressing these introductions.

'If we employ a sector strategy, we will find ourselves in endless conflict situations'

Up to this point, I haven't seen any of the law firms I work with find themselves in a conflict situation as a result of following a sector strategy. Admittedly, it might be slightly more challenging in some areas – for example, for patent attorneys as there is an obvious conflict in protecting the innovations of direct competitors – but even then, firms can usually circumvent that risk of conflict by looking more laterally at a sector.

For example, if a client is pursuing the automotive sector there are only a small number of car manufacturers, but there are an enormous number of companies producing the different parts these manufacturers need to use. Conflict can be avoided by mining these tributaries.

Conversely, if you look at clearly defined sectors like education, the attraction for the client lies in their advisers' total understanding of their particular sector. They want people who understand schools as, despite specific nuances between the individual schools, their needs are broadly the same. In these cases, the fact that their lawyer of choice works for a number of schools is very much viewed as a positive rather than a negative during the selection process.

Generally speaking, as long as the firm is not acting for a direct competitor or for a company the target is in a current dispute with, the risk of having to pass up an opportunity due to conflict is no greater than it would be from traditional marketing or business development.

'A sector strategy will have a negative impact on the way we currently market'

Sector marketing is not meant to replace time spent with clients and referrers; it should co-exist with and complement time spent with clients and referrers. Your clients in your chosen sectors will provide the background knowledge you will need to implement your sector strategy and generate introductions to both potential clients and to the relevant events and publications. Meanwhile, your referrers could have specialist teams in the areas you target. Using your current contacts to broker introductions to their specialists will cut a huge corner for you. Moreover, these introductions will be made on the back of existing goodwill, which will speed up the response and make the meetings themselves warmer, more enjoyable, and more productive.

'If we employ a sector strategy I will lose my existing clients'

No you won't… as long as your client relationships are as strong as they should be. The truth is your established clients come to you because they like and trust you; just because you now promote a speciality in charities, media companies, or agriculture is irrelevant as long as you provide the quality of service and quality of advice your clients deserve.

It may not sit comfortably with some partners, but if the concern is that promoting a speciality may damage existing client relationships, then the cracks in those relationships may run deeper than the client partners are willing to admit. In fact, if your client relationships are strong, it is likely they will have a proper think about who they know in your chosen sectors, which will lead to an increase in the relevant introductions coming from your clients.

'Fee earners are already busy, a sector strategy will just generate more internal meetings'

The idea is not to increase the number of meetings you have, but to ensure that the meetings you do have are the right ones and are effective. Sector marketing allows you to concentrate your efforts on more focused BD activities that actually make a difference. In fact, a side benefit is often improved internal communication across practice areas, which in turn should create more cross-selling opportunities – a barrier that still exists in too many law firms.

'A sector strategy won't improve our marketing'

The move from simply attending events where you are surrounded by competitors and unable to offer more to client conversations than a legal perspective will be replaced by events full of clients and potential clients – events where you can underline your suitability as the attendees' lawyer of choice by making a wider, more relevant contribution to the conversations being held.

Deciding which events to attend, what your level of participation should be, and how best to follow up will be much clearer (and cheaper and less time consuming). At the same time, you can underpin this 'face time' with commentary and articles placed in the relevant trade publications.

Many firms chase nationally recognised titles like *The Grocer* or *Estates Gazette*, but this can prove (at best) expensive and (at worst) fruitless. It is far more effective to concentrate on the myriad hyper-specialist monthlies that exist and are crying out for equally specialist legal editorial.

Eight cast iron benefits of adopting a sector strategy

Hopefully, these counter-arguments have convinced you that sector specialisation could be helpful in terms of winning more new clients. However, there are also some concrete benefits associated with adopting a sector strategy that shouldn't be discounted either. These include:

1. You will immediately appear more client focused, which means the firm will be more attractive to potential clients;

2. Your obvious understanding of the client's world will reduce their risk in instructing you, which means a higher rate of conversion and an easier conversion process, which will also reduce your current cost of sale;

3. You will be able to charge a premium (or at least harder rates) because of your perceived sector specialisation;

4. You will see marketing become easier as you begin to fish in the right ponds, away from competitors still marketing/networking in the same old places through inertia;

5. You will see a higher return on the time/money/effort invested in marketing and business development, which will reduce the time fee earners need for marketing, giving them more time for billable work;

6. You will increase the returns your business development activities generate because your fee earners will be approaching more relevant/enjoyable activities with more enthusiasm;

7. You will reap the rewards of first-mover advantage as many of your competitors won't have realised the opportunity sector-based marketing offers; and

> 8. You will be better able to leverage those sectors in which your firm already has a strong track record.

Choosing the right sectors

This is obviously the crunch part of the process. If you don't get your sectors right, the chances that your marketing efforts will succeed will be reduced significantly. When we look at potential sectors with our clients, we apply the following criteria.

1. In which sectors do you have the strongest track record?

First of all, do you actually have a strong track record in that sector? Do you have clients in this area you can cite as relevant examples while you're out in the field selling your expertise? You will also need to draw on these clients' knowledge of the sector to find out more about the events, publications, and associations that underpin it. You will also need to ask them for testimonials and for their permission to publish case studies you can use in your promotional activities.

Steel city

The bulk of the traditional client base of one of the firms we work with in South Yorkshire is – unsurprisingly, given their location – manufacturing businesses, so this was the first name on the team sheet when they sat down to work out which sectors they wanted to pursue.

Some of the partners raised an eyebrow, unsure of why there was such an unswerving desire to pursue this sector. After all, their client lists didn't have any manufacturing businesses on it, so why were all the others so keen to push forward with this sector?

That was the problem. They had thought of their personal client bases, not the firm's. A quick look at the highest billing clients showed that the firm was not only very strong in the sector, but also that the sector contributed a significant portion of their annual billings. Moreover, the deep-rooted personal relationships this volume of work had generated made sure that:

- Those involved had a working knowledge of the work required;

- Those involved knew how best to satisfy that need; and

- Those involved had enough contacts in the sector to make getting the team up and running much easier than it would otherwise have been.

2. What are you interested in?

Are there fee earners inside the firm with a genuine interest in the sectors you have chosen?

Interest will create a real and infectious enthusiasm which will rub off on targets and make you a much more attractive and credible option. Interest will also enable fee earners to find the time they need to keep up with the articles, discussions, and news they will need in order to demonstrate they are immersed and up to date with developments in their sector.

If you cannot show a genuine interest, you will just be another lawyer looking for work.

Eating and drinking in the south-west

One of the teams we worked with in the south-west of England loved going to the growing number of craft food fairs being held in the region. As they had some experience of working with one or two of the regular exhibitors, they chose food and drink as one of their sectors.

Because they had a genuine interest, attending the events outside office hours wasn't a chore, and once they were there that interest ensured they were not shy to start conversations with the various small businesses they came across. They rolled their sleeves up and got involved, trying drinks and tasting the various delicacies, and then they made sure they got the stall holders' email addresses so they could stay in contact.

The result was both groups (lawyers and stallholders) got new clients, and because the resultant relationships went both ways, the fee earners involved also enjoyed an additional layer of referrals from the entrepreneurs they had connected with at the shows.

3. Which sectors offer opportunity?

Are the sectors you've chosen big enough to support the level of fees you want to generate? Is there a good spread of likely targets? Not just in terms of the organisations obviously central to the sector, but also in terms of a generous supply chain of related and supporting businesses.

Is there a real likelihood the sectors will continue to grow? Or a danger that they may be in decline? Do the sectors have a real need for a range of regular legal support? Or are they likely just to need one-off work in just one or two areas? While track record and interest are essential components of a successful sector strategy, there is little point in continuing if there is no clear commercial opportunity.

Going green

In the case of pretty much every industry sector, the over-arching umbrella name we know that sector by is almost always inaccurate. Take technology for example, no technology business calls itself a technology business. They are a software developer, a nanotechnology manufacturer, or a bioscience specialist. The same can be said of the energy sector.

One of the firms we work with recognised that and, having realised they had a number of clients that could loosely be banded together as 'energy' companies, they began to drill down. Their research showed them that it was the renewable energy sector that promised the greatest potential for growth – something that was supported by their geography which leant itself well to being developed for the production of wind energy. Nor did it hurt that their local news had been led by fracking decisions and protests for some time!

Their energy team became their *renewable* energy team and the differentiation has allowed them to identify a number of publications, events, and networking groups dedicated to the green side of the energy market. The fact that all of these vehicles are more specialist and therefore not as well known has meant they are the only legal advisers present, and therefore they have managed to position themselves as specialists and quickly win a series of clients as a result, wins that have injected impetus and enthusiasm into some of the firm's other sector teams.

How do you build an effective sector team?

If you are to implement your sector plans effectively, you need to ensure the team you pick has the blend of skills required to cover every part of your plan. A combination of people – however enthusiastic they may be – who have a similar set of skills will leave some crucial areas uncovered, and that will restrict the success you achieve.

So, what skills will you need? As has already been mentioned, I split them into four areas:

1. **Writers** – These are the people who will put together your articles for the relevant trade publications and websites. They will also be responsible for blogging and for putting together e-shots and/or e-news bulletins if you choose to include these types of activities (which of course you should).

2. **Speakers** – These are the members of the team who will deliver talks at relevant events. However, they have other uses, including delivering training to clients and targets and running legal clinics at places where you know a large number of targets will gather.

3. **Schmoozers** – These are the people who will take responsibility for networking – of both the formal and informal variety. Traditionally, these will probably be the people viewed as 'rainmakers' or 'marketers', but they will not succeed in isolation. Without the other three groups' profile-raising activities, they will not have the level of awareness they need to really get taken seriously at the first point of contact.

4. **Diggers** – These are the people who will undertake the desk research, finding out what the relevant publications, conferences, networking groups, and trade bodies are. They'll also be responsible for keeping a steady flow of industry news coming into the team from Google alerts, RSS feeds, and online information subscription services.

In the next part of the book, the mini-masterclasses, we will look at each of these roles in much more detail.

Part 3:
Mini-masterclasses

Mini-masterclass 1:
Networking

Right off the bat, I'm going to be very clear about one thing – networking is not about going to networking events. Networking is the process of building a credible and productive network around you and there are many, many ways to do this.

Of course, this mini-masterclass will include some practical tips to make sure that, if you are going to attend networking events, you get something back from them. However, we will also look at the other ways you can use your particular skill set and your personal preferences to build a personal network without ever setting foot at a formal networking event.

Five things to remember so you establish the right mind-set

Networking isn't everyone's cup of tea, but – however you approach it – it is a mainstay of any lawyer's business development. If you are going to get something back from the time you invest in building your personal network, you need to approach it in the right way. Here are some tips to help you get into the right mind-set.

1. Remember: it's a science, not an art

'Art' conjures up an image of something innate; a talent or ability you either have or you don't. A science is something with rules: something you can learn, pick apart, and understand.

Networking is a science and anyone can learn the right skills, strategies, and tactics to succeed at it, and adopt them as part of their preferred way of working.

2. You don't have to 'work the room'

There is nothing more awkward to watch than someone 'working the room'. As they shuffle from person to person or group to group swapping cards, somnambulating through their rehearsed elevator script, you can almost feel the forced, counterfeit sincerity – and forced, counterfeit sincerity does not nurture relationships.

Networking is about human interaction. It's not about working people; it's about chatting to them.

3. You have to be there

As Woody Allen once said, '80 per cent of life is just turning up'. Yes, you have to place yourself in a position or situation where you are likely to meet the right people, but you don't just need to be there physically, you need to be there mentally.

You need to:

- Be mentally alert;
- Listen more than you talk;
- Ask open questions;
- Focus on the person you are speaking to;
- Ask about their interests, their family, where they go on holiday;
- Ask what they like doing outside of work; and
- Identify common ground you can use to start creating a genuine conversation.

4. Be prepared

You don't have to have been a boy scout for this one. Do your homework. Who's going to be there? Where is it? What is the purpose of the event? If you are going for the first time, is it OK to go with a colleague? Is there a dress code?

The better prepared you are, the more relaxed you'll be; and the more relaxed you are, the more likely it is that people will gravitate towards you, which means you will get more out of attending.

5. Appearances matter

Just like your mum always told you, remember clean finger nails and shiny shoes. You only have one chance to make a first impression so do yourself justice and make it a good one. If you don't make a positive first impression, it can take numerous subsequent encounters to alter the initial evaluation. If you turn up looking the part, it'll also help you to relax at the event.

Five ways to get the very best return from any networking opportunity

1. Set yourself goals

Identify clear goals ahead of each event and keep a mental checklist. The goals need to be clear, concise, manageable, and measurable. Have a system to showcase your successes and keep it going so you know how many contacts you're actually making. This will boost your confidence and enable you to adapt your style and structure appropriately so you generate even better results.

2. Be strategic

Most lawyers think they are short of time so you need to be strategic. Only choose the events with opportunity, the ones you know your targets are likely to attend. That way you'll maximise the likelihood of a result. In identifying the right opportunities, bear in mind:

- We make time for people we like and trust, and if we feel they will reciprocate;
- We make time for people who make us feel good; and
- We make time for people we can derive benefits from, and if we think we can also add value.

If the attendee list of the event you're looking at ticks these boxes, you'll meet the right people.

3. Don't be too strategic!

Don't forget that you can 'engineer serendipity'. New contacts can be anywhere, and are often only uncovered by a totally unquantifiable combination of savvy and total accident.

Remain open to networking opportunities in everything you do because you are constantly in contact with people who may need legal advice or will know others who do. And because these conversations are not strictly in a 'work' context, they will often be easier and more enjoyable.

4. Think about your existing clients

Do you have existing relationships you could leverage? Don't focus solely on looking for new clients; take time to look at your existing clients. Some will clearly be able to make referrals and introductions for you, but some may have hidden opportunities.

The more time you spend with someone, the better you'll know them; and the better you know them, the more likely it will be that you will identify additional areas where you could do more work together.

Similarly, your clients will know which events are attended by their peers rather than by professionals. Take the time to ask them which events they go to and which they consider to be productive or a waste of time. This simple line of questioning will help you uncover new arenas which will be target-rich rather than packed with competitors.

5. Look for introducers and facilitators rather than matters

Someone with a strong existing network has the potential to introduce you to multiple new contacts and, as those introductions will be made by a friend, they will be warmer and easier to progress and ultimately convert.

Use this as a model for your own networking too; offer added value by making effective introductions to your contacts.

Networking is all about expanding your contacts without increasing your overheads... and, after all, it's good to share!

Now take five...

Before you move on, take five minutes and write down:

- Two goals for your next networking event;
- Two places that could prove useful for meeting new contacts;
- Two clients you could ask to suggest events you should be attending; and
- Two introductions you could make between contacts in your network (including colleagues).

Four ways to plan the conversations you'll have

Whether you choose to go down the traditional networking event route or adopt a strategy based on putting together smaller groups, if your networking is going to be successful, you need to have something to say. Here are ways to make sure you do.

1. Recognise your personal strengths

Think about all of your positive past experiences. What has gone well and why? In what circumstances do you connect well with people? Who has made a positive impression on you and why? Who have you made a positive impression on?

Then make a list so all of those points are front of mind and ready to drop into the right conversations at the right time.

2. Think about your 'targets'

Who are you going to/likely to meet when you get out of the office? What are they likely to want and/or need? How can you help them with those demands? Do you know others who could help if it's not your field of expertise?

Again, having all of this front of mind if/when the opportunity arises will make you more credible and more attractive in the eyes of the people you talk to.

3. What can you deliver?

Have a think about examples of previous clients or projects that could increase your new contact's understanding of your value. What problems did those clients have? Better still, how did you resolve them?

4. Think about how you introduce yourself

Elevator scripts are bad. Without exception. They are truly awful mechanisms. All that over-rehearsed fakery does is mark you out as (at best) a 'professional networker' or (at worst) a total phoney.

However, you do need to introduce yourself so have a very short one-liner that puts you and the skills you offer into focus and in a way that will grab your contacts' interest. For example, if you're a tax lawyer, don't say you're a tax lawyer; say you save your clients thousands of pounds each year. If you're a litigator, don't say you're a litigator; say your job is to help people resolve arguments with the outcome they want.

Then (very, very) quickly divert attention away from you by asking the person you're speaking to what they do.

Now take five…

Before you move on, take five minutes and write down:

- Your two key personal strengths;
- Two ways you could help the people you're likely to meet; and
- How you actually do help people – this will become your introduction.

Five things to remember once you're in a conversation

1. Create rapport

If you are going to establish trust, you need to be interested in the individual first and their business second. If you're approachable and sincere, you'll create a favourable impression and, as with all things, 'likeability' is key.

2. Share contacts and knowledge

At the event, be prepared to open up your contacts; it will mark you out as someone who genuinely wants to help and will enable you to build credibility quickly.

3. People don't like being sold to

Especially if they've never met you before, so always think 'conversation'. Believe me, the 'flogging' euphemism is no coincidence when people are talking about selling, so don't leave everyone you meet feeling flayed alive after you've spoken to them.

4. Don't appear desperate

Develop the relationships *before* you need them and nurture them over time. Stay in touch, go for coffee, keep talking, and steer the relationship so that when an opportunity does present itself, you are best positioned to take advantage of it. Don't push your services onto your new contact; you'll only end up pushing them away and leaving them with a very poor impression of you.

5. Remember to collect business cards

Business cards are valuable. They are the tangible result of networking so don't forget to collect them. And once they've been collected, don't just stick them in your pocket. Make a quick note of anything interesting or salient on the back of them. Jot down any agreed follow up. Make a note of a holiday, bar, or restaurant they mentioned, or of their children, partner, or sports team. Then leave them on your desk because it's time to follow up…

Ten ways to follow up

While there are a million ways to network, there is only one way to turn networking into work and that's to follow up. The trouble is that follow-up is all too often the bit lawyers find difficult. Here are 10 tips to make follow-up a little easier.

1. Leave your foot in the door

Whether you're finishing a conversation at a networking do, a coffee, a beer after work, or a lunch, you need to leave your foot in the door; you need to make sure you have a legitimate reason to get back in touch and stay in touch to keep the conversation going.

My preferred phrase is 'what I'll do when I get back to my office is… '. That 'is' might be to send them some slides, an article, or an introduction to a colleague, client, or contact. It doesn't matter. All that matters is that they'll be expecting you to get in touch and know why you are.

2. A quick email

After you meet someone, you're immediate, in-built physical reaction should be to send them an email. It doesn't have to be long – in fact, it can be really short – but it needs to be sent.

If you've followed step one, you won't be scrabbling for focus, reason, or content; but if you do need a steer, the template I suggest to clients is:

Hello Contact,

Good to meet you at x event yesterday. I trust you enjoyed it as much as me.

I will be in Contact's Location on 3rd and 9th May and would like to see if we can meet up for a coffee to learn more about

Contact's business/practice. Would you have 45 minutes in either day?

If this doesn't work, perhaps you could suggest an alternative towards the end of June as I'm planning another visit to Contact's Location in six or so weeks later.

Thank you.

3. The LinkedIn handshake

Although an email is the preferred immediate follow-up mechanism, it is becoming more and more acceptable to send a LinkedIn invite instead. Just make sure you personalise their rather anodyne template and include a mention of where you met... and why you want to stay in touch.

4. Be definite about dates

As you will have seen form the template I have just shared, the best thing to do in follow-up is to adopt an either/or policy when it comes to suggesting a next meeting. People react better to this and are more likely to come back positively if they have a definite choice. If you leave it open ended you're making it harder for them, which in turn will make it more likely your request will be rejected or ignored.

It may be that neither option works, but at least you are earning yourself an opportunity to make a third suggestion that probably will suit your contact.

5. That promised introduction

One of the best ways to leave your foot in the door is to promise an introduction. If you do offer it, make sure you deliver and deliver quickly. Again email makes this easy. My suggested template is:

> *Hello Contact,*
>
> *It was great to meet you last night. As promised, I wanted to put you in touch with Third-Party Contact because I think a chat would benefit you both.*
>
> *By way of introduction, Contact is a partner at ABC accountants and a specialist in the technology sector.*
>
> *Third-Party Contact is the MD of XYZ Software Ltd and is heavily involved in the local creative hub.*
>
> *I'll leave it to you both to follow up, but please let me know how you get on.*

6. Something from your archive

I'm guessing that your firm is publishing some sort of content somewhere, whether that is articles, updates, or more general opinion pieces and blogs, and whether that is on the firm's website, LinkedIn, or internal newsletters. If something sticks out from your conversation that ties in to something in your back catalogue, you can either attach it to your immediate 'glad to meet you' email or use it a few weeks down the line as an excuse to get back in touch.

7. Use your firm's social calendar

If you have an event, workshop, legal update, or seminar coming up, invite your new contact to attend. Exposure to the invited audience will probably be of benefit and it gives you an opportunity to talk but not be tied to them for the duration.

8. 'Saw this and thought of you'

Yes, that again!

9. Lack of response isn't lack of interest

Train yourself to realise that the reason you haven't had an immediate response isn't because your contact isn't interested in you, but more than likely because of client pressures, something tricky that's landed on their desk, the fact their email server went down, or their boiler at home is on the fritz.

Keep going. Tenacity (at least evenly spaced out tenacity) is flattering rather than irritating, and the right people will appreciate your efforts.

10. #banter

I've left this to last for a very good reason. I know the majority of lawyers reading this will dismiss it out of hand because they won't think it's appropriate. However, for those amongst you who do meet someone with whom you share a common interest or an immediate connection, try to be brave enough to have a bit of common or garden banter with them.

It may be about your favourite types of film, about the sports team you both support, or about somewhere you've both been on holiday or a restaurant you both like to eat at. While it may seem a bit over-familiar, this is by far the most fertile foundation upon which to build a genuine – and productive – long-term relationship.

Now take five...

Before you move on, take five minutes and:

- Write out your template for your follow-up email and save it somewhere where it will be instantly accessible; and

- Familiarise yourself with your firm's social and seminar calendars;

- Familiarise yourself with the content you have available to use as a follow-up attachment.

Five alternative ways to network

The key to successful networking is doing what you and the people you want to see/meet/get to know better want to do and are comfortable doing. You can literally do anything and if what you want doesn't exist, create it.

Here are five more innovative networking initiatives I have seen clients successfully put into practice.

1. Come dine with me

One client we worked with in north-west England found networking difficult, but she realised she did have a core of four or five referrers who were invaluable to her practice. She also found out that they all shared a liking for cooking.

The client set up a 'come dine with me' arrangement where they'd meet every couple of months at each other's houses for a nice meal and a chat. Needless to say, all of the work they had to refer was referred to those around the table.

2. Five-a-side football

A commercial/IP lawyer we worked with in south-west England started a five-a-side football team made up of his key referrers – all were of a similar age – and entered the local league. They then had to meet up once a week and had an opportunity not just to work together in a non-work context, but also to sit down and have a drink and a chat afterwards while they got their breath back.

3. Beer tasting

Over the last couple of years, Kelham Island in Sheffield has enjoyed something of a renaissance and new craft beer pubs are opening up all the time.

One of our clients has used the new venues (and their ever-changing wares) as an excuse to get some likeminded contacts together to sample new beers and have a chat in the type of informal setting they prefer.

4. Film club

One of our London-based clients doesn't like the more male-orientated, drinks-based approach to networking so instead she set up a film club. Thanks to the fact there are a number of cinemas in London that specialise in showing classic films, they have managed to work through quite a catalogue of 'must sees' or 'must see agains' and then go for a coffee and cake afterwards to discuss the films they've just seen.

5. Plus one

Another Yorkshire-based client has set up a series of quarterly 'plus one' events with a few trusted friends. Basically, the managing partner in question teams up with a barristers' clerk and a couple of well-connected local businessmen, chooses a date and a venue, then they all bring a plus one. By changing the plus one each time, this has allowed the four members of the group an opportunity to grow their networks in a warm and informal way.

Now take five...

Before you move on, take five minutes and:

- Identify one alternative venue, activities, or place you would enjoy using to meet up with your contacts;

- Identify one event going on in your town or city that you think would offer good networking or hosting opportunities;

- Write down three clients, contacts, or colleagues you think would enjoy going to both; and

- Invite the corresponding list to the venues/activities/places and events you've identified.

Your 'cut out and keep' guide to networking

If you are going to generate the maximum return from your networking activities, always remember:

- Be smart;
- Be approachable;
- Have focus and clarity of purpose;
- Do your homework – 'be prepared';
- Be confident and positive;
- You have something of worth to offer so don't 'work the room', relax and enjoy the experience; and of course
- FOLLOW UP, FOLLOW UP, FOLLOW UP!

Mini-masterclass 2:
Presenting

Five facts that will help you get into the right mind-set to present

1. Your success hinges on your ability to engage your audience, not on your ability to provide technical information;

2. Your audience will forget the majority of what you say (however well it is delivered), but they won't forget you so be open, honest, and likeable;

3. Know exactly what you want to happen after your talk and add a clear 'call to action' to make it as easy as possible for your audience to do what you want them to;

4. Preparation is key – there are three aspects to this:

    i.   Planning;

    ii.   Delivery; and

    iii. Follow-up;

5. Don't benchmark yourself against others in your firm or in the legal profession – aspire to be like those presenters from outside the profession who you have seen and enjoyed.

Eight ways to make sure your presentations actually deliver a tangible return

The trap too many lawyers fall into is rushing to produce their slides rather than planning the structure of their talk thoroughly before they move into the production stage. If you invest more time in thinking about what your audience wants to know – and will benefit from knowing – and then clarifying exactly how you will deliver both successfully, you will achieve far better results (and produce far better slides).

When it comes to planning, always consider:

1. What action do you want people to take after your talk?

All too often, I hear people say 'my talk is just for information' or 'it's just a profile builder'. No, it isn't. You want to make people do something specific afterwards so that you keep the conversation going and stay visible. Make sure you offer a few options on your last slide and make sure those options are clear.

You could:

- Offer to email slides in exchange for a business card;
- Offer a free special report or white paper on a similar topic to that covered in your presentation;
- Offer a free initial audit of a relevant part of the audience's business or a free initial consultation if you are on the private client or family side;
- Offer a chat over coffee to allow the members of your audience to delve deeper into your topic on a one-on-one basis.

And always, *always* end by saying: 'I will be staying on for coffee/lunch afterwards and you can find me at (x) where I will be happy to discuss any questions you may have so please come and say hello.'

2. What is the profile of your audience?

Before you start putting your presentation together, ask yourself:

- Who is attending?
- How many will be attending?
- What approach (formal or informal, progressive or conservative, creative or technical) will people expect?

- What will the demographics (age, nationality, job title) of the audience be?

All of these answers will dictate the style of your delivery and the style of your accompanying materials.

3. What is your audience's current level of understanding when it comes to your topic?

Is your talk for beginners, intermediates, or experts? Again, the answer will dictate the content of your presentation. In cases where there will be senior and junior attendees, it is often worth running two sessions with slightly different content so you totally engage and build credibility with those at both ends of the scale.

4. What can you find out about the venue you'll be presenting in?

Know your venue and, if at all possible, visit the room in which you will be presenting in advance to get a feel for the place. Some of the key things you should be finding out on that visit are:

- Are there projection facilities?
- Will you need to bring your own laptop on the day, or send slides in advance?
- What will the room layout be? Cabaret is best for big groups, but horseshoe is best for small.
- Will there be technical support on the day?
- What are the acoustics like? Will you need amplification equipment?

5. What is your host's preferred delivery format?

Don't make any assumptions – ask your host, client, or audience how they like their speakers to communicate. PowerPoint is one possibility, but there are many others, for example:

- Talk without slides. This is a great way to build a closer emotional connection with the audience, but it requires confidence. Get it right and you will win (i.e. David Cameron in the Conservative leadership election); get it wrong and you will lose (i.e. Ed Miliband in the recent UK General Election).

- Use props. This works particularly well for more complex technological explanations and for specific product launches.

- Experiment with alternative visual presentation tools like Prezi.[1] These are all great software packages, but require you to know how to use them. Also, check with your host that the package is compatible with the available IT.

6. Always mail your presentation electronically in PDF format

This tiny tweak will better protect your intellectual property and make your slides look more professional (resolution is sharper in PDF). It also ensures you avoid any potential formatting issues if your hosts have different versions of PowerPoint.

7. Do you know your audience already, or do you need to establish your credentials?

Ask yourself if it is really necessary to share your professional biography at the start of the talk. Often, these intros can be quite dull so should be avoided, especially if the audience knows you already or if your entire career history is not relevant to your talk. However, if the answer is 'yes', just use your relevant credentials (key clients, memorable matters, association or trade body membership) and present them in a memorable way that grabs the audience's attention (timelines, mind maps, and plenty of images and logos).

8. How can you start to interact with your audience before your talk?

When it comes to making your talks more successful, getting buy-in is half the battle. You can make this easier by getting in touch with your audience before the day of the talk by:

- Asking the audience members what their key challenges or needs are in advance by using a simple email questionnaire;

- Asking key stakeholders to give their input as to what the key issues are over coffee before you start designing your talk; or

- Asking your audience what they want you to cover before you start, though admittedly this option is probably one for the confident amongst you!

Seven ways to inject more impact into your presentations

1. Have a strong start

As the magnificent Curtis Mayfield once said, first impressions last forever (arguably, an early example of subliminal marketing; his band was called The Impressions). People will form their opinion of you in the first 30 seconds and rarely budge from that position, so make sure you have a strong start and you deliver your opening confidently.

One tip I received when I used to present internationally to professionals in the shipping world was to walk around the block a few times before my slot to go over and over the opening two slides in my head so I had the words ready to deliver verbatim. This allowed me to start more confidently and that confidence helped me get off on the right foot, which improved the delivery of the remainder of the presentation.

2. Do you sound enthusiastic?

People are more likely to believe what you say if you look like you believe what you are saying. However, people are also more likely to get distracted and get their phones out if they're forced to endure a mumbled monotone.

3. Does the way you present yourself fit with your message and what you're selling?

If you are selling high-value services, do you dress smartly and look the part? Conversely, if you're selling to a third sector audience, do you dress *too* well?

4. What are the three key messages you want people to take away from your talk?

Peoples' ability to retain information from talks is very poor so keep it simple; make sure your audience remembers three points. You can even underline those points further after the event by providing more detail by email or in a hard-copy hand-out.

5. How engaging are your slides?

Bin the bullet points and use 'words in windows' (two or three words in a box) instead. Use images, schematics, charts, and diagrams in preference to words wherever possible. Keep sentences short. And always, *always* make your fonts *BIG* – those at the back need to see too.

6. How will you keep people attentive for the duration of your talk?

People have poor concentration spans. After 18 minutes, there will naturally be a dramatic drop in your audience's attention. Here are some things you can do to help your audience remain focused on what you're saying:

- Use a variety of media, e.g. props and video;
- Use different ways to communicate, e.g. visual, aural, kinaesthetic, and numerate;

- Have breaks; and
- Involve the audience via questions and exercises.

7. Tell stories

Stories are an opportunity for the presenter to show the personality behind the suit.

Stories will also help you to establish more of a personal connection with your audience; people relate to stories because people like stories (they're significantly more interesting than bullet points too). This increased personal connection will help your audience recognise why they will need to see you and continue the conversation after your talk.

On a more physical note, when you tell stories you are dipping into real memories which means you can recall the detail without having to look at the screen behind you. This makes it much easier for you to continue to strengthen your connection with your audience because you can maintain eye contact throughout.

Now take five…

Before you move on, revisit an old presentation and ask yourself:

- Did it have a strong start?
- Did it meet the information requirements and level of understanding of my audience?
- Did it have three key points for my audience to take away?
- Did *I* have a strong start?
- Did the slides visually engage the audience's attention, or overwhelm them with text?
- Did I vary delivery and employ different techniques to hold my audience's attention?
- Did the presentation end with clear calls to action?

Five physical changes you can make to your delivery to immediately improve your presentations

1. Rehearse, rehearse, rehearse… and rehearse out loud!

How many times have I heard 'do I *really* need to rehearse my talk? I am very busy, you know…'. 'Yes' is the simple answer (at least if you want it to be any good). Rehearsal removes glitches and will improve how confidently you present on the day of your talk. There are no buts and no exceptions!

2. Manage hand-outs efficiently

Always distribute any materials *after* your talk, never before. In the event you are forced to provide some form of hand-out before you speak, never share the actual presentation, just offer some pertinent background information that will put your talk into context. You want people to listen to you. If you give people a hand-out, their reflex action will be to read *it* rather than listen to *you*.

Crucially, sharing materials afterwards will make it easier to keep the dialogue going. Don't have hard copies; stick to electronic formats. That means you have to send it via email. An email exchange is the perfect way to start building visibility, and the required contact details are the perfect way to build your marketing database.

The other thing is if you produce your slides properly (fewer words, more images), they won't be particularly helpful without your commentary. You should really have two sets of material:

● Slides that are visually rich and text-light; and

● Something to be emailed later that is more detailed and text-heavy.

3. Invest in a mobile clicker (and use it)

Have you ever been to a talk and seen someone bending down to click the mouse on their laptop? It doesn't look great, does it? Thankfully, the solution is readily available and has a dual benefit; it will also allow you to be kinder to your back! That solution is to buy a remote clicker from amazon or your local electronics store.

4. Don't hold your notes

Your primary objective is to engage your audience; holding notes presents a barrier. There are also two other big reasons why you should never hold notes:

- If you are nervous, you will shake your notes and this will unsettle your audience. They will start to have doubts about what you are saying as the fact that you look unsure of your subject will not inspire their confidence.

- Looking at your notes will stop you from making eye contact with your audience. Again, you need that eye contact if you're going to build trust and form a genuine connection.

5. Burn the lectern!

Standing behind a lectern is another barrier between you and your audience. That barrier makes it harder for you to engage people. Have the confidence to step away from the lectern and speak to people in a more natural, conversational way.

Two ways to follow up and make sure your presentations turn into instructions

Many people are disappointed by the results their talks, seminars, and workshops generate. While there are many explanations for poor outcomes, by far the most common is inadequate (or, more accurately, poor) follow-up. So, how do you follow up to maximise the value of the time that you have invested in your talk?

We've already looked at 'calls to action', so let's look at how to use multiple marketing touch points to help you stay visible after you have finished your presentation.

1. Set yourself very clear (and measurable) objectives

'Win business' and 'build profile' are neither clear nor measurable; they're woolly and lazy. Instead, you need to have ODEs:

- O is your optimum result. That could be that targets come up to you voluntarily and enthusiastically after your talk to ask you to visit them at their offices.

- D is your desired outcome. That could be a warm round of applause and that you've delivered your calls to action clearly enough that 25 per cent of attendees email you with requests for more information or to take you up on one of your offers.

- E is the essential. You didn't freeze, you got to the end, and five people came up to ask for your slides.

2. Variety is the spice of BD

Business development success will not necessarily come from your talk in isolation. Success comes from the combination of all the things you're doing to keep visible in your chosen markets. Aside from giving your talk, you need to think about:

- How best to communicate across different channels (e.g. print, social media, email, and face to face) because everyone prefers a different way of communicating; taking a copy of the attendees and 'linking in' with all of them after is an easy way to start the ball rolling.

- The fact that buying professional services is largely about timing; if you don't maintain a variety (and consistency) of touch points, you'll drop off your targets' radars so that when an opportunity arises it won't be you they think of.

- Whether prospects might want to see other people in your firm before making a decision; follow-up allows you to introduce those other people.

- How to maintain your coffee (or indeed green tea, craft ale, sparkling wine, or organic smoothie) contact with clients, referrers, and business targets – in that order of priority. When it comes to coffee, systemise and measure the contact so you stay on top of it... and stay visible.

- What the *right* networking events are (i.e. the ones your competitors don't go to, but your clients and targets do). And, as we agreed in the previous chapter, don't just attend – participate, then follow up within 48 hours.

- Possible speaking platforms, and how you can use all of the checklists in this mini-masterclass to make sure your presentation is the most engaging.

- Opportunities to build a relationship with the organisers so you get repeat bookings.

- How you can use Google Alerts and RSS feeds to build a catalogue of 'saw this and thought of yous'.

- Case studies and client testimonials, and make sure you use them liberally as a reason to get back in touch and show clients and prospects you have all the necessary credentials.

Now take five...

Before you move on, take five minutes to think about the next talk you're due to give and write down:

- How you're going to make sure you'll generate immediate follow-up opportunities with some of the audience;

- How you will make sure you connect with all of the audience;

- How you plan to maintain contact with the whole audience;

> ● How you will identify which attendees you need to make more of an effort to get a personal audience with; and
>
> ● How you will get that personal audience.

Ten ways to avoid 'death by PowerPoint'

PowerPoint is a massively useful tool, but one that has garnered bad press through misuse. That doesn't mean you shouldn't use it, but if you are going to use it, please make sure you:

1. Don't put your logo and livery on every slide. The first and last is enough.

2. Don't use bullet-points. They're dull and they make the audience read them instead of listening to you.

3. Use more images. People will pay more attention, interested to find out why you've used them.

4. Add in blank slides. They'll remind you when to explain things in more detail.

5. Don't use standard templates. Everyone's seen them and they weren't that good to start with.

6. Drop the boring blue backgrounds. Use white backgrounds, experiment with greys... just don't under any circumstances go white on blue!

7. Sit back and look at the design. Do you like it? No? Then the audience probably won't either.

8. If you're not a natural designer, look at TV, magazines, billboards... See what's popular; it's popular for a reason.

9. Don't have too many slides. Rehearsal will tell you if there are too many, but as a general rule two minutes to one slide is a good ratio to work with.

10. Don't use technology, transition, and animation. It's one more thing that can go wrong.

Eight ways to improve attendance at your firm's seminar programme

While all of the practical suggestions in the preceding checklists have equal applicability to giving talks at an event organised by your firm or by a third party, there is also a need to look more closely at your firm's seminar programme.

One of the things we hear frequently from law firms is that attendance at their self-run events is dropping. There are reasons for this (rise in available material, especially online, an increasing scarcity of time, alternative and usually electronic delivery mechanisms), but that doesn't mean the information you want to impart is any less valuable or that seminars should be dropped from your marketing and business development.

Here are some tips to help you get your seminar programme back up and running:

1. Set clear objectives

It may look as though I'm over-egging this point a little, but if your seminars are going to be successful you need to know why you're doing them. 'Because we always have' is not a reason to run seminars; the following are sound commercial objectives:

- To engage with the professional community – your referrers, introducers, and intermediaries;

- To promote a particular sector experience to an audience of prospective clients;

- To mix current and prospective clients to run through a relevant legal update (and give your clients an opportunity to say good things about you over the tea and coffee);

- To boost your profile in a new geographic market or industry sector;

- To open you up to a new audience as a result of hosting with a trusted partner; or
- A little bit of all of the above.

2. Choose the right subject

If you are spending time with your clients (on either a general or a sector basis), as we discussed earlier in the book you will know exactly the type of legal advice and support they and their businesses demand.

You will also have a much clearer understanding of the specific issues they face and the pressures they are under. And these aren't legal issues; these issues will be commercial, economic, or social.

When you put those two sets of information together, you will know what to cover and how to package it in an attractive way for your audience. Why will it be more attractive? Because it will actually address the issues your audience faces, which means attendance will deliver real value. And if you get that right, your attendance levels will grow.

3. Choose the right format

Setting tighter objectives will help you choose the right format for your event. Generally speaking, the default for a law firm is a traditional 'chalk and talk'. You prepare slides, then stand at the front of the room and present those slides to an audience sitting in neat rows of seats. In many cases, this works fine… but not in every case.

For example, if your objective is to strengthen ties with a smaller, more targeted group of professionals, it may be worth considering a facilitated 'round table' discussion. Writing a loose agenda based on the hot topics of the day and inviting an accountant, a property agent, an IFA, a patent attorney, and/or a banker's perspective to complement your own will allow all parties to put their views across, and it will mean that they leave with a much more comprehensive understanding of the topic(s) you have discussed.

If your aim is to mix targets and clients from a specific industry sector, a smaller, more informal group may work better and allow you to encourage much more audience participation. You can also add in a few more breaks for tea, coffee, or sandwiches than you might for a more traditional presentation to give attendees more of a chance to mix. What's more, you should pick your audience strategically; if you know someone who makes wheels, invite and introduce them to someone who makes tyres. From a more mercenary point of view, a smaller more conversationally based group will also make it easier for your clients to expound your virtues to your prospects.

And then there are the e-formats. No one likes doing webinars, but they do get around the perennial problem of persuading people to take the time out to come to you, and they give you an impressive back catalogue you can promote separately to allow people to view your content at their convenience.

4. Always follow the two golden rules

Firstly, make your seminars practical rather than academic. Whoever you invite, make sure the content you deliver guarantees they leave with more knowledge than they came in with. More importantly, make sure that the extra knowledge they leave with can be directly applied to benefit their businesses or, in the case of private client-focused events, their lives.

Secondly, make sure your events are as engaging as possible. Choosing the right format will help, but if you are going traditional:

- Use your best speakers;

- Book guest speakers you've seen before and know are good; and

- When it comes to your slides, use pictures, stories, and movement to hold your audience's attention.

5. Get the invites right

Every campaign begins with invites, and your invites need to look good. A recipient's first impression will make their decision as to whether they'll attend or not, and if the first impression is that the invites have been cobbled together with every expense spared, their impression will be that the content and delivery will doubtless follow suit.

Make sure you employ a bit of design. Make sure the copy succinctly captures the benefits of attending.

6. Get the invite list right

Again it is a generalisation, but far too many firms still rely on the same base lists for every event. They then wonder why attendance has fallen through the floor. A seminar – and, more to the point, the success a seminar generates – is inextricably linked to the strength of the invite list.

If you are targeting a specific sector, do some online research (online directories are a wonderful thing). If you're looking for credible local targets, use the open source lists of growing or best-performing businesses; ask referrers if they will suggest relevant names for you to add to the list.

As with all things in life, the more you put in, the more you'll get out.

7. One size doesn't fit all

To generate the highest possible level of acceptance, you need to try a bit of everything because people react to and respond to various media in different ways:

- Hard-copy invites should be followed by emails and replicated on your website;
- Links to that page should be broadcast by all members of staff using social media platforms and, where possible, followed up with personal emails to well-chosen contacts; and

- Don't just send it once – send it two or three times. Like you, your target audience is busy. Your invitees might miss your first and second attempts but respond to the third because the topic is of interest.

8. Put in a little additional effort

Don't rely on automatic responses to your invites. Take a look at the invite list and pick out 10 people: good referrers or clients you have identified as having real development opportunity who simply must attend. Then divvy this list up amongst the team behind the seminar and phone these must-haves personally.

It may seem time-consuming, but each call will probably last only two minutes and the personal touch will boost acceptance levels by almost 100 per cent, not to mention it will give you a valuable opportunity to reconnect with your most regular referrers.

Now take five...

Before you move on, take five minutes to think about a seminar you are about to/want to run/should be running, and write down:

- The main objective for running that seminar;
- The three key points you want to get over during your presentation(s);
- The profile of the audience;
- The best format for that audience;
- How you are going to run your invite campaign; and
- How you plan to follow up.

Your 'cut out and keep' guide to presenting

If you are going to generate the maximum return from presenting:

- Set objectives;
- Have three key points to deliver;
- Have a strong start;
- End with clear calls to action;
- Text-light, image-heavy slides;
- Know your audience and construct your content accordingly;
- Be confident, engage, and keep eye-contact;
- Don't create unnecessary barriers (e.g. notes or a lectern);
- Inject some enthusiasm; and of course…
- FOLLOW UP, FOLLOW UP, FOLLOW UP!

References

1. Established in 2009, Prezi is a cloud-based presentation tool which is growing in popularity as a more dynamic (but less structured) alternative to PowerPoint. Instead of moving through slides in a linear fashion, with Prezi you put all of your content onto a single canvas and then the browser zooms in on each item in turn, based on a path you have chosen.

Mini-masterclass 3:
Writing

As the internet continues to play an increasing role in both keeping people up to date and in positively influencing the major search engines, the old adage that 'content is king' has never been more true. And tomorrow it will be truer still.

If you are going to create sustainable visibility and become more visible to the people you want to know you (but currently don't), you will need to create a library of content to back up the face-to-face BD you are doing.

Three reasons you must engage in writing
1. More opportunities for more fee earners to get involved
Writing allows those who may be technically excellent but more reticent about the face-to-face side of marketing the opportunity to engage in BD and create a profile for themselves while they help the firm create work-winning levels of visibility.

Moreover, many hands make light work. Having more people to distribute BD tasks amongst will make it easier for those more naturally attuned to the networking and social sides to pursue those activities, safe in the knowledge that the content required to support and further their activities and take care of the online side is in production.

2. 101 applications
Once you are producing written content, there are myriad ways you can put it to work for you. For example, it can be:

● Added to your site to underline your credentials and boost your SEO;

- Sent out as part of your e-marketing;

- Used as an attachment to show you are active/expert in the area covered when you follow up by email after meeting someone;

- Cut and pasted into your LinkedIn profile as an update (a function that immediately notifies your contacts that you have posted something so there's an immediate visibility benefit);

- Promoted via the other social media platforms to drive traffic to your website;

- Repackaged as slides and used as a workshop or onsite training vehicle; and

- Used to prove to external editors that you can write so you win new slots in new publications.

3. Currency and credibility

Having something to say about relevant topics shows you are on the ball and that you know your stuff. More importantly, if you take the right approach (and more of that later in this mini-masterclass), it shows you know how to apply your knowledge to your clients' and prospective clients' circumstances so that they gain the highest value from instructing you.

For the professional services, this is an absolutely essential part of the purchasing process. As I have said before, the decision a client makes to appoint a lawyer is based on their ability to mitigate risk. If you can prove – in writing – that you understand what's going on, what affects your market, and exactly how you can help clients to successfully navigate those issues, you will strip away some of the layers of doubt and persuade them you are a credible option.

Now take five ...

Take five minutes and:

1. Assess the different ways you could distribute content using your firm's current marketing infrastructure;

2. Choose a topic you could write about that you know would benefit your target market (whether that is a client or a professional contact);

3. Write down two recent legal developments concerning that topic;

4. Write down how those developments could affect your target market;

5. Write down how your intervention/help/support would prevent those outcomes;

6. Write a short piece of content following the model you've laid out in steps two to five;

7. Distribute that content using the mechanisms you identified in step one; and

8. Rewind and repeat – you now have a personal content marketing model!

Seven potential publishing platforms

Once you come to terms with the fact that producing content is a 'must do' rather than a 'could do', the question I am usually asked is: 'Ok, that's fine but where do I get published?' Generally speaking, the answer splits into seven:

1. Your firm's website

Whether it's a blog, an article, a brief update, some form of commentary on recent events, or a more formal white paper, you need to be constantly updating your website. If you don't, you will lose ground on those of your competitors who are, and

I really can't think of a firm I've come into contact with who is not actively pursuing one or more content marketing initiatives (I *can* think of many who should be doing much more, but that's a different story!). And because there are a variety of options, there is no excuse not to get involved in the one that suits your personality and style best.

Have a think about your practice area and your current client base and put together the framework that suits them best. Make sure you are not only producing good content, but making it available in the way that suits your readers' preferences. For example, a private client practice should be marketed at individuals so content needs to be short, easy to read, and designed to explain situations and next steps clearly and concisely. For SEO and stay-ahead-of-the-competition reasons, it also needs to be updated regularly. This means a blog may be the best way to go.

However, if your audience is business owners in a particular industry sector, you may want to use a more detailed approach. For example, listing practical solutions to common problems using case studies alongside your technical know-how. In that case, downloadable white papers may be the best route to take.

2. Social media

While Facebook and Twitter are good ways to promote what you have produced to the audience you are building up, what I am really thinking about here is LinkedIn. As I've already said the 'Publish a post' functionality on LinkedIn allows even the most inexperienced and least confident user the opportunity to publish something (written specifically or reproduced from something the firm has published elsewhere), and then sit back while the site tells all your contacts you've published something. Better still, the whole LinkedIn community can search for and find your posts. This could make you visible to an audience you would otherwise never meet.

The only suggestion I would make here is to think about how people use LinkedIn. It will almost certainly be on a phone or tablet, and it won't be as part of an in-depth research exercise. This means you need to keep it short, readable, and to the point.

3. The trade press

One thing we have found out from working with sectors of all shapes and sizes is that there is literally a title (online or hard copy) for every niche – and, indeed, every niche within those niches. We will look at this in more detail in the next mini-masterclass, but do not be afraid to contact editors if you have a good idea you think would benefit their readers. In the main, they will be happy to publish the thoughts of (i.e. practical advice from) professionals who specialise in their fields.

4. Via trade associations

Trade associations are a massively underappreciated and over-looked commodity, and I've never understood why. They are directly relevant to the audience they are set up to service, and if that audience has direct applicability to your practice, they are an open conduit to the people you want as clients. And as with the trade press, there really is a body for every sector and every type of person and/or professional.

They also have newsletters, websites, and online repositories crying out for content; and when you match that to their desire to give as much help to their members as they can, you can see why they could potentially be a pivotal part of your personal BD plan.

5. Via your contacts' vehicles

Do your contacts, clients, and referrers have websites, portals, or newsletters? If they do, then your contribution could be as welcome as it is valuable. Offer to write something for them (therefore making it easier for them to fill up column inches and save them the hassle of chasing contributions from within their own organisations) and ask for it to be linked to your site.

6. The local press

Again, we will look at how to use the local press to best effect in the next chapter.

7. Your own blog

There are a number of dedicated blogging sites, like WordPress, that allow a budding author to publish content and reach a potentially global audience (as long as it's all tagged correctly). This could be a way to reach people you may not even have dreamed might be interested in what you have to say.

Now take five …

Take five minutes and:

1. Think about who your clients are and the ways each grouping is most likely to receive information (the easy way to do that is to take a piece of paper and write the client types down the left and then the mechanisms – and it will always be more than one – on the right).

2. Go to the next point ('Three things to remember when you're writing') so that the finished product is in the most relevant and engaging 'voice'.

3. You now have personal media plans for each type of client. Stick to them when it comes to producing and distributing content for them and you won't go far wrong.

Three things to remember when you're writing

At Size 10½ Boots, when we interview clients on behalf of law firms, the two things we are told they want from their lawyers are:

- Someone they get on with, don't feel awkward contacting, and feel comfortable discussing some fairly major and unsettling subjects with; and

- Someone who will give them straightforward, practical advice and not hide behind overcomplicated sentences and legal jargon.

And to give praise where it's due, over the last decade the lawyers we work with have definitely become much better at the softer touches. More and more are willing to chat on the phone, meet up for a coffee, drop by a client's office, or offer more social, 'personal interest' based, events.

The only trouble is, in the majority of cases this new found informality and sociability doesn't extend to their written content. Now, I understand that as lawyers from the start of your training you are taught to look for detail, to recognise the nuance in the text in front of you, then cleverly to use that detail and nuance to your clients' advantage. The only trouble is, nuance and detail don't make very entertaining reading.

Going back to what it is that clients and referrers want – someone they get on with and someone who will give them straightforward, practical advice – what do you think the best way to tick those two very particular boxes might be? That's right. It's to provide some straightforward practical advice that people can actually use in the plainest of English.

If you want to produce content people will: a) use; b) enjoy; and, most importantly, c) respond to, here are the three key things to remember:

1. Don't be afraid of how you speak

When was the last time you used 'thereby' when you were in the supermarket? When did you last say 'ergo' when you were out for dinner? Exactly, always write as you speak… you can even use abbreviations!

In the same way that there is nothing more off-putting than a blog or an article that is written like a thesis, there is nothing more engaging than a piece of practical advice that comes across like a friend (or acquaintance if friend is too close to the knuckle and erodes into your professional service sensibilities). Imagine you are talking to a friend and replicate the language and points of reference you would usually use.

2. 'In your shoes' beats the letter of the law every day
The people who read your content want to know how to tackle something that directly affects them; they don't want to build up a working knowledge of the law. Always make sure the advice you give is practical and straightforward and don't sit on the fence, try to add some clear direction even if that direction is to get in touch with you to discuss it further.

Also, try to use anonymous examples and/or case studies to put your advice in context. People respond well to stories and the more you can frame your advice within a situation the reader has faced or is likely to face, the more likely it will be that they will get in touch with you at some stage.

3. A sense of humour is not a sign of weakness
Too many lawyers are still a little scared of sharing a bit of themselves, especially when they're writing. However, without any real data to hand, my experience has been those that are willing to use a slightly lighter touch and inject some humour are generally busier than those who still find it awkward.

Now, obviously I'm not talking about producing a stand-up routine every time you write (and I'll be the first to admit that, by definition, divorce, employment tribunals, and the Companies Act don't lend themselves to comedy!), but I am talking about using a lighter touch overall. Perhaps you could employ a little exaggeration, caricature, or slightly more creative points of reference.

Coming back to the results of the various client research programmes we've run, clients say point blank that they want an adviser with personality and who they feel totally at ease with. What better way to show you fit that particular bill than writing with your tongue (at least partially) in your cheek?

Three ways to conquer writer's block

Now we've looked at why you have to write and where you can write, the next question we may need to tackle is: 'What do I write about?' It's a valid question. Your content will only do what you want it to if it is practical, relevant, and leaves your readers feeling more informed having read what you've written than they did before they read it. Likewise, your content will only gain traction (and have a positive impact on the search engines if we're being cynical) if it is produced regularly.

So, how do you come up with enough topics to maintain that level of consistency? How do you avoid the time-wasting tedium of sitting and staring at a blank screen while you wait for inspiration to come as the publishing deadline your head of department gave you creeps ever closer? Well, I'd split it into three approaches, which if you blend and vary them will make it look like you are a natural.

1. What are the latest developments in your field?

This has to be the most obvious because, after all, the purpose of your content is to underline that you are an expert to those who are interested in your field. However, as it's probably going to be the most technically focused route to inspiration, it should be the one you use most rarely.

Limit your coverage of the latest legal updates to those that really matter and those that are most relevant to your practice/clients/targets/contacts. Don't get too technical. Avoid legalese and jargon, and always explain your point in absolute layman's terms because people will be put off if you use overly technical language, and over time they will come to associate your content with that style which will eventually put them off reading what you're writing at all.

2. What do you talk to your clients about most regularly?

What issues are your clients bringing up when you talk to them? What questions do they ask you when you meet? Which areas do they ask for your advice on most regularly? What situations/sets of circumstances do they ask for help with most frequently? The chances are that if these are the issues that affect the minority, they'll probably be of interest to the majority so all are potential blogs, articles, or email alerts. And if you aren't having those conversations, then jump straight back to Chapter 4 and reboot your approach to client development!

3. What's in the news?

The news is a constant source of inspiration. There are two approaches:

1. Take something that's happened that relates directly to your area

For example, the media has run blanket coverage on the unfortunate story of the pensioner who was allegedly hounded to death by charity fund raisers. This has developed into strong calls for the whole regulatory structure monitoring charities to be overhauled and strengthened. If you are involved with the charity sector, you could question whether stricter regulation will solve the problem or whether it is a deeper lying issue.

2. Take something that's high in the public consciousness and make it fit your area

For example, if you are a family lawyer you could follow up a high-profile celebrity divorce with a piece outlining the pros and cons of pre-nups (while positioning yourself as the go-to person to write that pre-nup, of course). However, ask yourself one question: Will everyone else not be doing the same thing? Probably, so if you're going to stand out you need to be a little more creative.

When Branislav Ivanovic was bitten by Luis Suarez, one of our clients ran a piece outlining what to do should one of your employees report an incident of 'oral assault' by another employee. OK, even in the wacky world of employment law this is unlikely to be a regular occurrence, but it did generate enquiries because it was: a) all over the news; b) a way of promoting the need to act on any case of assault in the workplace; and c) it was quite funny (the article, not the biting).

4. Use popular culture

I know I said there were three ways to beat writer's block, but in truth there's a fourth. The reason I've snuck it in at the end is that it takes a little more confidence. If you can take something from popular culture and give it a bit of a spin to make a point that relates to your area of expertise (preferably with a bit of humour), that can not only enable you to make your point, but also to engender a bit of reader loyalty because people want to be entertained. It is also a sure-fire way to increase your pass-on rate, which will bring you to the attention of new prospective clients. More importantly, it will also help you mark yourself out from those of your competitors who are still wedded to the traditional po-faced technical approach your readers neither value nor enjoy.

Now take five...

Take five minutes and jot down:

1. The two issues you are coming up against most frequently at the moment;

2. The three things your clients/targets/contacts need to know about those issues so that they aren't affected by them;

3. How you could frame them in a more entertaining way (using something from the news or from popular culture); and

4. The deadline by which you will write a short piece on each using your three learning objectives and the new points of reference.

Mini-masterclass 4:
PR – Become an industry expert

By Sharon Cain, managing director of Quest PR and former BBC and Sky TV journalist

Now that you have conquered writer's block and established that there is a wealth of collateral you can draw on to engage with – and communicate to – your target audiences, this chapter focuses on how you can harness this content to be highly visible as an industry expert.

Becoming acknowledged as a thought leader across traditional PR and social media leverages your profile and elevates your firm above its competitors. Achieving this goal does not happen overnight, nor does it entail constantly generating copy – which is not a viable option anyway due to fee-earning pressures.

Success is secured via a robust, relentless, and disciplined process which entails compiling a bank of strong and interesting content that can be tailored and rolled out across an integrated marketing, PR (traditional and digital), and social media programme – for maximum impact.

Harnessing the tools to become a thought leader across PR and social media

Below are some examples of PR tools to draw on. Each one is effective in its own right and the tools you select should be those which dovetail most closely with the firm's overarching strategy.

PR tools

1. Expert comment

The previous mini-masterclass highlighted some potential publishing platforms to accelerate visibility. It also gave pointers on writing about topical issues aligned with your sector expertise. Remember that *you are the expert* when submitting articles on current issues, trends, or impending legislation across your target media. Also, don't be afraid of making predictions and giving forecasts. In 15 years of running a PR agency, a journalist has never queried a client's forecast we submitted.

2. Piggybacking the news agenda

Becoming a media 'go to' who producers, reporters, and editors call on to comment on topical and salient issues is a powerful measurement of success. It requires the media understanding which are the critical issues and areas you can comment on – and you reacting fast if an opportunity arises. Just as when I worked in national and regional broadcast organisations, today's media still approach interviewees who provide the best interviews/soundbites.

Before approaching broadcast media, ensure that you are media trained – because you only get one chance (see tips further below). As mentioned elsewhere in this book, setting up Google Alerts is vital to avoid missing opportunities.

3. Profiling

This can include 'softer' features (be discerning as to which ones you select) which convey your personality, approachability, and your sense of humour (see Mini-masterclass 3). Profiling can also give you and your firm an edge over your competitors – counteracting the 'suited and booted' perceptions.

4. Articles in trade media

There is a wealth of trade media covering product and service sectors – spanning exporting, manufacturing, retail, food, and leisure to name but a few – which will welcome articles providing they are new, topical, and interesting.

Being published in key media read by your clients reinforces their confidence in your expertise and that of your firm. It can also help to influence prospective clients in a competitive pitch, and hyperlinks to your articles can be included in e-newsletters.

5. Press releases

The most frequently used tool in the PR toolkit, press releases are also excellent for increasing visibility in a highly competitive environment. The myriad press release topics available to you include deals and commissions, new appointments to show you are recruiting and expanding, winning awards for growth, customer service, innovation etc., along with charity and fundraising activities to reflect your firm's values and ethos.

6. Award submissions

Winning and being shortlisted for awards are proven time and again to open doors and drive sales. As with all PR tools, it is vital they are meticulously researched to ensure they underpin the wider strategy. For example, if a goal is to attract top talent as your firm grows, Best Employer awards are key. Scooping accolades as a niche law firm can likewise showcase your expertise – and attract referrals from full service practices.

7. Speaking opportunities

Speaking opportunities constitute another powerful platform on which to present tips, advice, and insights at networking events and trade associations, where respective organisers will promote your presentation/seminar/workshop across their extensive databases. It is a given that being invited to present firmly places you as an expert in your field and you will be pleasantly surprised how presenting facilitates natural networking and follow-up opportunities as attendees approach you afterwards.

Tips on maximising value from the PR tools
A formula for writing effective press releases

Bombarded with hundreds of emails daily, journalists will spend less than 60 seconds deciding if they are going to use your story. Make your release newsworthy and follow this formula:

- Ensure the headline grabs attention – include it in the 'subject' line of your email;

- Get straight to the point and convey your story in the first paragraph;

- Ensure the release answers the who, what, why, where, when, and how;

- Keep it succinct and avoid jargon;

- Tailor the release to the style of the media (print and broadcast) you are targeting;

- Include statistics if possible – they make the release more palatable;

- Include your contact details and additional information in Notes to Editors; and

- Accompany the release with an arresting photograph – images from professional services can be dull so think laterally and inject them with energy and personality to make them stand out.

Steps to 'pitch' your thought leadership proposals to the media

Becoming a media 'go to' is dependent upon reporters and producers knowing the subject areas in which you can offer opinion and comment. Follow these steps for success:

- Prepare thoroughly by knowing the media you are targeting along with their differing needs. Research what they have previously written and review their profiles on social media.

- Send them a 'teaser' comprising your key areas of expertise and examples of how you could add value – i.e. making sense of impending legislation or explaining the implications of the outcomes of court cases.

- Before following up your 'teaser' with a phone call to reporters and producers, be aware of their deadlines, which differ dramatically for traditional media, digital, and broadcast media.

- If you manage to get hold of them, assume they won't remember your email so have it ready to send to them as you are speaking to them to increase your chances of engaging with them.

- If they sound interested in your email, let the journalist's response guide you to the next step in the process – e.g. they may commission a comment, article, or ask you to keep in touch.

- If you are targeting the trade media, obtain their advance features, which gives you a heads up on the topics they are seeking contributors for.

- Be prepared for knockbacks. If a reporter or producer is short with you, or simply does not have the time, don't be put off. They work to tight deadlines and are contacted by hundreds of PRs daily.

How to make your award submissions stand out

Writing submissions can be resource intensive; however, the business-boosting benefits of winning awards are innumerable. It is therefore important to bear in mind that judges, who invariably have busy day jobs and are tasked with dozens of entries to wade through, may not have time to read every word of your award submission. Follow these steps to stand out from the crowd:

- Only compile them if your firm/department meets the award criteria and can demonstrate growth, innovation, new services, etc. across the qualifying period.

- If available, study the content and format of previous winning entries.

- Dependent upon the submission layout, use sub-headings such as 'Department marks unprecedented expansion', 'Enhanced client services offering', 'Innovation pays dividends' to grab attention.

- Aligned with the above, spell out year-on-year expansion, profit, and staff increases.

- When compiling submissions, put yourself in the judges' shoes.

- If testimonials are required, give clients advance warning.

- If your work has achieved media coverage, be sure to include it.

- If shortlisted, maximise the milestone and promote the story via your social networks (traditional media only use stories about winners).

Maximising media interviews

The opportunity to be interviewed by a journalist – particularly now that there are fewer of them – is one to be relished and maximised.

The majority of interviews will be conducted via telephone, and as with all editorial opportunities – both print and broadcast – you have no editorial control over what messages the reporter will choose. I recommend the following tips:

- Find out the areas of questioning in advance – some reporters (trade and national media) will send questions in advance to keep the interview focused.

- Prepare six-to-eight bullet points of your salient messages.

- Listen hard – it's challenging to establish rapport over the phone.

- If you start rambling, ask the reporter if you can answer the question again.

- Most journalists understand the power of social media so let the reporter know (this is applicable across all positive media interviews) that you/the firm will share the published article/radio/TV interview across social media.

Handling radio interviews

Before appearing on national radio, it is advisable to harness the wealth of opportunities on the BBC's extensive regional network. Radio is a very personal medium so imagine you are talking to an audience of one. The techniques below will help you to feel confident and competent.

Pre-recorded

- Be prepared – research the programme, the presenter, and the topics being covered.

- Avoid preparing 20 bullet points – too many talking points will confuse your message.

- Use the soundbite – this is a response the reporter will select from your interview for the news bulletins. It enables you to get your message across, but remember it can be as short as 10 seconds.

- If pre-recorded, stop the interview and start again if not happy with your response.

- Be brief – keep answers concise and keep on track.

- Use plain English and avoid jargon.

- Remember, you're the expert.

- Paint pictures during the interview to illustrate examples of your responses.

- Covey your personality and message in your voice. Smile.

Live radio interviews

- Assume the mike is live.

- Listen hard.

- Interrupt when necessary.

- Live interviews can include phone-ins from listeners – best practice is to be civil to callers (even rude ones), write down their names, and take notes if you need to.

- Relax and enjoy the interview! If the interviewer likes you and receives good feedback, they will often ask you to appear again – success!

Handling TV interviews

Whereas radio is all about your voice and the words you use, TV is visible in every sense – and mainly reliant upon pictures. TV interviews are not necessarily about what you say – but about *how* you say it – so it's vital to exude energy and enthusiasm.

Pre-recorded TV interviews

- Ask the reporter questions about the angle and other interviewees.

- Talk to the interviewer not the camera.

- Stay still and avoid shuffling or nodding your head.

- Check you are happy with the backdrop of the interview – try to include the firm's awards, logo etc., in the background.

- Check hair, tie, jacket before the interview.

- As with radio, ask to stop the interview and start again if not happy with your response.

- Dress appropriately – plain colours, no fussy patterns, avoid jewellery.

Live TV interviews
- Do some breathing exercises.
- Arrive early to get used to the surroundings.
- Meet the interviewer if possible.
- Ask about the line of questioning – check how the interviewer will introduce you and ensure the information is accurate.
- Stay wholly focused and don't be afraid of interrupting the interviewer.
- With remote studios – establish telephone or sound contact, listen hard, look straight at the camera, assume you're on camera at all times – and don't leave until you're told it's ok.

Harnessing the tools to become a thought leader
Social media tools
In the same way that it is fundamental to know your target media for your PR campaign and to adapt your style to the respective regional, trade, national, digital, and broadcast channels – social media also requires an in-depth understanding of your audience.

Aligned with the emphasis on 'social', it is about communicating, sharing, and engaging with – as opposed to *selling* to – your audiences. Social media is necessary to ensure that you and your firm remain 'in sight and in mind'.

1. Blog
Businesses that blog generate more leads than those that don't. Blogs are a proven platform to showcase expertise and aforementioned collateral. In my experience, they increasingly act

as a thought leadership magnet for the media to contact you for interviews and comment.

How to engage your audience via blogs:

- Devise a blog schedule to stay on track.

- Launch your blog with three-to-four posts to gain some traction at the outset.

- As with your press releases, write an attention-grabbing headline – ask questions in blog headlines.

- Always include an image to match the headline – the headline and the image will either draw readers to your blog or send them to a competitor's blog that has more appeal.

- Ask your readers questions – you want them to engage with you.

- When pitching your thought leadership comment ideas to the media, include a link to your blog – your content can spark an idea for the journalist to write an article or feature.

- Stay focused and sustain content which is relevant and newsworthy.

- Incorporate video blogs into your blog schedule.

- Seek out guest blogs from key influencers who are pro-active and will share and promote your blog across their social media channels.

- Co-ordinate your blog with your Twitter feed.

- Post frequently – Friday morning is a good time and Friday afternoons at 4pm are deemed the most 'retweetable' time of the week, i.e. when followers are most likely to retweet your blogs.

- Include internal links to previous blogs.

- Use Google analytics to gauge which topics are attracting the most interest – and give your readers more of what they want.

- Avoid populating your blog with press releases – it will dilute the strength of the thought leadership collateral.

2. LinkedIn

Arguably the most powerful B2B marketing tool of the 21st Century, LinkedIn is pivotal to integrated PR and social media campaigns.

Mini-masterclass 3 has covered the importance of populating LinkedIn with value-added content and, on the premise that no-one is reading your PR, blog, and LinkedIn posts at the same time – LinkedIn enables you to:

- Share topical developments with your readers;

- Post your blog updates; and

- Maximise your rich blog content to ask questions and start group discussions.

It is important to ensure not every LinkedIn post is centred on the firm – because your engagement should be about the clients and not all about you and the firm.

Also, bear in mind that an increasing number of journalists qualify their interviews via LinkedIn so ensure your profile is the strongest it can be when they are checking you out.

3. Twitter

Almost 50 per cent of users who follow a business on Twitter are more likely to go on and visit the company's site.

Like blogs and LinkedIn, Twitter is also effective for organic SEO and a visual tool for maximising images, expertise, and personality across joined-up communications programmes.

As with LinkedIn, avoid populating your Twitter platform with a plethora of self-indulgent posts and provide updates of relevant breaking news stories along with articles and reports that are relevant to the sectors of your clients and prospects.

4. Facebook

Although Facebook may not be the most appropriate platform for law firms to engage with clients, it can be invaluable for attracting and recruiting top talent.

Dynamic and ambitious graduates will expect their prospective employers to have a Facebook presence. You will find many of the UK's biggest practices populating a vibrant company site with punchy posts which reinforce their commitment to training and developing their staff as well as sharing updates on their pro bono activities, milestones, developments, and PR successes – all of which enhance their desirability in a climate which is facing the worse skills shortage for years.

Achieving the joined-up formula for success

You will know that the integrated approach is successful and that you've achieved the 'Tell them, tell them you've told them – and tell them again' formula when:

- PR collateral and comment is adapted for blogs;
- Expert comment from PR collateral is used to start LinkedIn discussions;
- Blogs and PR coverage are shared via Twitter; and
- Your firm's Facebook site links to your 'Best Employer' evidence (awards/articles/training).

How to measure success

What gets measured gets treasured – so begin with the end in mind and establish at the outset exactly what success will look and feel like aligned with the wider business goals. Failure to do this will result in frustration and lack of clarity when evaluating your investment and ROE (return on engagement) from your campaign.

The Public Relations Consultants Association advocates putting the spotlight on the three Os:

- **Outputs** – activities taken place during the campaign;
- **Out-takes** – the results of the activities; and
- **Outcomes** – resulting changes.

Below are some key PR and social media measurements – not all of them may be relevant to your firm:

- Number of leads/approaches generated.
- Levels of client awareness.
- Circulation reach from PR articles, profiles, and interviews.
- Using advertising value equivalents (AVEs) – deemed by many in the PR industry to be controversial, AVEs are a method of calculating an equivalent monetary value if you had bought advertising instead of doing PR. It can be a helpful comparison for firms who have previously advertised.
- Google analytics – a basic free service to analyse your blog and website traffic. The tool provides an insight into who is reading your content, where they are viewing from – and what topics are attracting their interest.
- Twitter has recently launched its own analytics offering, which tracks engagement rate, mentions, retweets, new followers, interactions with each tweet, link clicks, and likes.
- Hootsuite is also an effective tool connecting all social media profiles in one place and enabling users to monitor, manage, and schedule posts.

- SumAll is a cross-platform marketing analytics tool combining social media, web traffic, and sales metrics data for businesses.

Now take five...

From the above, identify a combination of five PR and social media tools to launch your integrated campaign to become an industry expert.

Make a list of eight pieces of newsworthy content you will compile and then edit and roll out across your PR and social media platforms to boost visibility, profile, and reputation.

Mini-masterclass 5:
Research

The first four mini-masterclasses have dealt with what are usually considered the mainstays of business development – networking, writing, speaking, and PR. Now, we are going to look at the glue, the activity that binds them all together yet is often the easiest to forget – research.

Without a researcher on the team, you will not know:

- Where to network;
- Where to write;
- Where to talk;
- What to talk about; and
- What is happening in your markets so you can drop it into the conversation.

While the ultimate aim of this chapter is to look at what needs to be researched and provide some practical guidance as to how to do it quickly and efficiently, the first objective is simply to remind you that:

a. Research is an essential task that must be done if your BD is going to be successful; and

b. It is a task that can be given to the people who say they can't/won't get involved in BD so that they can make a contribution too.

Which seven things do you need to research?
1. Events
Events can take several forms, including:

- **Conferences** – These are invaluable as a source of new contacts (as long, of course, as your networkers are prepared to attend, engage, participate, and follow up), and of new business cards for your future marketing. However, conferences are also the source of a number of other valuable pieces of information. The outline of the speaker's presentations will tell you what the hot topics are in your local area, practice area, or sector. They will also have attendee and sponsor lists, which again you can use to bolster your marketing database, whether those additions are potential targets or potential partners/referrers/introducers.

- **Networking groups** – Again, these are invaluable sources of new introductions and a proven way to boost your word of mouth marketing strategies.

- **Exhibitions** – Personally, I always think that, given the limited amount of marketing time you have as a lawyer, walking round an exhibition isn't the most effective use of your time (and hanging around on a stand being ignored by the other visitors for three days *definitely* isn't), but again the exhibitor list will house some relevant prospects and potential contacts and if there's an associated conference programme that will provide insight into the topics you need to know about.

- **Social events** – Sometimes these masquerade as networking events, but to me they're slightly different. These are events that attract segments of professionals and/or commercial personnel, but rather than being a traditional card-swap, they are based around a specific activity or location because the audience the organisers want to attract are interested in that activity or location.

For some, these are much more attractive as they are less formal; and because those who attend tend to share interests, it is easier to start conversations when you're there, and to keep those conversations going (to maintain visibility) afterwards.

2. Groups

Again, groups can take several forms, including:

- **Networking groups** – We've covered these in the previous point, but what I'm thinking about here are the unofficial networking groups, the other areas of life people tend to band into. For example, meetings of school governors and charity trustees allow you to meet similar people in similar walks of life, all with personal and professional requirements for legal advice and all with contacts, family, and friends they can pass your name on to because they have requirements for legal advice. These groups tend to work particularly well for private client lawyers.

- **Sports clubs** – We have a client who funded the memberships for one of their teams to various sports clubs (golf, squash, running, canoeing) rather than traditional business networks on the proviso that they entered all the competitions (so they were paired with people they would not otherwise have known or spoken to). The result was an increase in direct and third party instructions because the fee earners were more enthusiastic, more comfortable, and turned up much more regularly than they would have done to other, more formal events.

- **Other groups** – For the less sporty, there is a limitless supply groups for every interest. As long as you give your researcher(s) a decent brief, they will find them. And of course, as I have mentioned earlier in the book, if the group you want doesn't exist, start it!

3. Associations

Trade associations and industry bodies are a rich but rarely mined seam. As long as you pick the associations most relevant to your practice area or chosen sector, they can give you access to their membership (all of which will be a potential target or referrer).

However, they also run conferences, events, and training which provide you with additional opportunities to speak and network and they tend to run websites, information repositories, and publications you can contribute to. They are also usually affiliated with other associations which you could use to fuel the next stage of your BD plan.

4. Publications

Nowadays, there are publications not just for a niche within a niche, but also probably for niches within those niches. Our research for clients has led us to some titles that cover subjects we never knew existed, never mind knowing if there were publications covering them!

One thing that all of these publications have in common is a need for editorial and, as we looked at in the writing and PR mini-masterclasses, as long as your researcher finds the right targets and the insight to ensure you can demonstrate you will provide a practical, informative, and relevant angle, you are likely to be commissioned.

5. News

Although it's down at number five on this list, news is arguably one of the key things to gather. It will influence and inform every marketing decision you make (what to write about, what to blog about, what to tweet, what to include in speeches, what to run seminars on) and guide every conversation you have with the targets, contacts, and clients in your sights.

From a credibility point of view, it is essential you are seen to be current, informed, and able to discuss the issues of the day, whether – depending on your practice area and/or target area – they relate to the opening of a new charity shop locally or the most involved issues influencing international currency transactions.

6. Stats

While news is obviously an essential component, statistics and studies can add another dimension. Many sectors – geographic as well as industry – regularly produce reports and studies that uncover growth and decline trends and set out what to expect in those areas over the next few years.

Many industry bodies and other professionals (most notably accountants) are also involved in publishing this type of study, so monitoring new sources could also allow you to identify and progress potentially valuable referrers and introducers.

Not only can this improve the written content and presentations you put together, it can also allow you to spot future opportunities early, something that can often give your team first-mover advantage so that you can act before your competitors.

7. Gossip and hearsay

What is reported is sometimes not as useful or attractive as what hasn't been. Whatever field people are in, they want to know what is being whispered about so, if you can, find online discussion forums that are hinting at what is likely to happen or what is rumoured to be happening. If you can drop that into conversations with contacts and targets, you will immediately be more credible and, arguably, more useful.

A good starting point for gossip and hearsay are the groups on LinkedIn. While they are unlikely to provide ground-breaking or potentially seismic shifts in your target markets, they will probably steer you towards a scrap of news or train of thought you can employ to appear more informed and more credible when you're in conversation.

Now take five…

Before you move on, take five minutes and write down:

- Who in your department or team will be doing your research;
- The activities each member of the team has committed to doing; and
- The type of information each will need to succeed.

What are the 11 best sources of information?

Thankfully, it is no longer necessary (as it was when I started as a cub salesperson in the 1990s) to walk down to the local business library and plough through the directories in its reference section to find out the who, what, and where in your sector. The internet has given us almost instant access to any piece of information we might want – all at the click of a button, and all without any investment other than a (very) little time.

Time, you won't be surprised to hear, is the only argument we now hear when it comes to why research hasn't been done, but it is a feeble excuse. One search only takes a fraction of a second (literally, Google will confirm just how small that fraction is every time you hit send), and the results can be cut and pasted into any format in little more time. As long as you are managing your time correctly, a quick search here and there will not impinge on your fee-earning time.

With regards to where to look online, the following tips should help you to cut down your search time even further:

1. Google

For those amongst you who think this should be entitled 'search engines' or 'online searches', my challenge is: which other search engines do you use? Exactly. 'To Google' is now a verb because it's the only search engine people use.

Simple Google searches are now the fastest way to research anything and should be a researcher's first port of call. And don't be happy with page one. Because of the way the Google algorithms work, the subsequent pages also have some gems, and even if they're one-step removed from your original search parameters, they can often be just as valuable.

2. Online telephone directories

When I was young, the telephonic world was encapsulated by and limited to huge great directories that arrived at pre-defined points during the year with an ominous thump. Thankfully, these less-than-easy-to-use tomes have now been consigned to the memories of people who are as old as me, replaced by faster and more user-friendly online versions.

Again, for some reason, these free and open-to-all tools are all too often forgotten, which is a travesty because they are exceptionally useful when it comes to building a marketing or target list.

If you were interested in, for example, dentists in Chorley, all you need to do is log on to an online directory like Yell.com (other alternatives are available), enter dentists in box 1 and Chorley in box 2, and click the 'search' button. Within seconds, you will have a list of targets you can cut and paste into your target list – adhering, it goes without saying, to the required privacy and opt-out rules when you come to market to them.

3. Trade associations

We have already looked at why trade associations are an invaluable part of any comprehensive marketing plan, but one thing to bear in mind if this is a group you would like to progress is that membership lists are usually (quite rightly) fully protected so the greatest value you are likely to get from an association's website in the first instance is their aims (so you can double-check they are right for you), the profile of their membership (ditto), and perhaps some insight into or latest news from their area of influence.

However, the website should also include who to contact to begin a conversation and how to get hold of them, which is marketing gold in itself.

4. Websites run by publications

The websites run by publications are a researchers dream. They not only provide the headlines and summaries of the articles in the current editions, they can also house:

- Extra content (blogs, columns written specifically for the site that don't appear in the main publication);
- Constantly updated news sections;
- Email summaries of content and related news that you can sign up to for free;
- Any special reports they may have published;
- Back issues packed with useful information;
- Lists of advertisers;
- Lists of events;
- Relevant industry links (to associations and key industry figures); and
- Links to the other publications in their stable... all of which will provide you with everything listed above too!

Just as importantly, they will also have a full listing of their editorial staff so that you can pick out the best contact and get your writers to begin a conversation.

5. Websites run for conferences

The websites run for conferences and other industry events are pretty similar to those being run by publications, except the key reference sources are:

- The attendee list (if it is a conference);
- The sponsors of the event;
- The exhibitor list/floorplan (if it is an exhibition);
- The speaking programme and the precis of the talks being given; and
- Links to the other events the organiser is running in the areas you are interested in.

And again, take note of the organisers – specifically, the person responsible for the conference part – and make sure the speakers in your team are starting conversations that could end up with them speaking at the next event.

6. Independent, commercially run info-sites

While these are not widely different to the websites run for/by publications, the fact that they are run almost purely for advertising and advertorial purposes means that they are often a great source of lists of the people involved in your market. As those listings are put together for advertising purposes, they also contain fairly comprehensive contact details, which is an additional benefit of fishing in these waters.

They also tend to be highly populated by product information and press releases. These pieces of information are also useful as they will give you more to talk about when you are in conversations with the people within your markets – marking you out as the informed and up-to-date option – and give you a steer as to what direction your market is most likely to take, which again will allow you to recognise and take advantage of trends early.

7. Social media

As we've already discussed, the discussions going on in LinkedIn's groups are a good way of gauging what people are talking about and concerned with. However, don't discount Twitter or any of the other popular platforms, which all have the own strengths.

If you take Twitter as an example, news is instantaneous and continual. People are constantly adding, sharing, and highlighting news and commentary from sources you might otherwise have missed or been impervious to. Keeping an eye on these feeds is a simple way to allow news to come to you for reuse and redistribution.

In addition, many firms and industry figures are now arrogating these (again, using free and widely available apps like Flipboard) to make their own social media newsletters with little effort or time required.

8. Directories

If you are still adamant about making that trip to the library, you won't leave empty handed. Most reference sections still offer a variety of resources that can prove extremely useful, including hard copy directories.

While the internet will house the lists you are looking for somewhere, hard copy directories are often better laid out and easier to use. You may, however, have to prepare yourself to fall back into the dark ages. Many libraries will not let you photocopy entire sections so you may need to take a pen and paper and do it the old way.

9. Back issues

Libraries also usually hold back issues of the publications you are interested in (both trade and local press, depending on your interest and practice area).

From a lead generation point of view, these will have display and classified ads (all of which are potential targets) and the details of past authors (all of which will either be targets or potential contacts).

Moreover, a quick scan will allow you to see the perennial subjects that the publications keep coming back to (and how they have been tackled by those considered industry experts or in the other professions that support the sector). These are the bankable topics, the ones that you should concentrate on when it comes to writing, speaking, and organising your own programme of events.

10. Special reports

Although the reports available at the library are no different to those you will find online (i.e. the ones we covered under point six in the first part of the masterclass), the fact that they are in hard copy makes them easier to read!

The fact that libraries will band these reports together by sector/industry regardless of the publisher or source means it's easier and quicker to delve deeper to find out more information or gain an alternative perspective. They will probably also be stored with past issues of the same report, which means you can make comparisons, something that again will help you to identify key trends.

11. Press releases

Most libraries will also hold a selection of press releases. Again, as with the commercially run infosites, these are useful in terms of providing trends and developments you can drop into conversation when you are with your target market.

Now take five...

Before you move on, take five minutes and:

- Revisit your list of the members of your team, the activities each has committed to doing, and the type of information each needs;

- Write down the best sources for each piece of information they require;

- Assign personal responsibilities to the person or people who will do the searching; and

- Set a deadline for each.

What are the four golden rules for any researcher?
1. Currency
If you are positioning yourself as an expert in a particular sector or as the 'go to' person in your local area, you have to be current. Don't report things late, and definitely don't report things that have changed (or are likely to change) since you came across them. The aim of reporting and using current points of reference is to establish your credibility and mark you out from your competitors. If you are reporting after them or, worse still, half-baked or even erroneously, that will not happen.

The good news is, increasingly, user-friendly content management systems, email, and social media allow us to report instantly, and often without even having to turn on a PC.

2. Consistency
Just as important as being first is being consistent. Research is a stand-alone job because it needs to be executed consistently. If you are posting content and sharing news, it cannot be done in spurts. If you have a run of news, then go quiet for a month or two, then pick up again, you are starting from scratch because you will drop off your clients', contacts', and targets' radars as quickly as you climbed onto them.

Make sure you have as much information coming to you as you can arrange to cover busy times, and make sure you have holiday cover if/where necessary to keep the wheels turning when your researcher is unavailable.

3. Communication
Every cog in your information-gathering machine needs to have an objective. Once you have set that objective, the best means and frequency of reporting their findings will present itself, for example:

- **Conferences/events** – Unless they are imminent, this could probably be an agenda item at a monthly or even bi-monthly departmental or sector team meeting. Attendance (not to mention budget) needs to be sorted out in advance, so it's best to maintain as long-term a view on the relevant conferences and events as is possible. The other advantage of discussing options in a meeting is that it makes it easier for the speakers and networkers in your team to put their hands up to take personal responsibility for signing up for or pursuing a possible speaking slot at the events your research uncovers.

- **Networking groups** – Again, it's probably better to add these to your team meetings for the reasons outlined above. Over time, though, a calendar of relevant events can be built up and managed via a shared drive (once people are used to remembering to look at what's there and are actively volunteering to attend... and are used to reporting back on successes, opportunities, and new contacts at your meetings) using a simple spreadsheet that shows the event, the venue, the date, and the person who will be going.

- **Speaking opportunities** – This can be done personally on an 'as and when' basis. Your researcher(s) would be personally responsible for telling the speakers what is on and who to contact (maybe alongside intelligence on what to offer to talk about, using the newsfeed side of your research to improve the likelihood your offer is taken up), and the speaker would be responsible for reporting progress and follow-up.

- **Editorial possibilities** – As with the speaking events, but the leads would be passed to the team's writers, who in turn would be responsible for reporting progress.

- **News (and links to news)** – Relevant industry reports (for trends, stats, and future developments) and articles (for 'saw this and thought of you' email contact) can be forwarded at any time. Similarly, links to any useful or relevant news can be forwarded at any time so that the team can have a look at the headlines and use the links themselves for LinkedIn updates and tweets.

4. Creativity

Sometimes, your first search won't yield the results you want, so be prepared to try different (but related) words in your searches and employ a little bit of creativity to find alternative searches. For example, if 'employment professionals networks' doesn't get any hits, 'HR managers groups' might; or if you don't find anything under 'travel logistics magazines', you might under 'haulage magazines UK'.

One thing I can be absolutely sure of is that there is at least one magazine, event, association, and website for every single commercial or personal niche in the UK and you will find them as long as you're prepared to be a little flexible in your searching.

LinkedIn is a live database these days. If a company's website doesn't give the name of their CEO or FD, it is worth running it through LinkedIn. Similarly, if you find relevant groups (by industry or geography), you will see:

- Who is participating;
- Which companies/organisations they belong to;
- What they're talking about;
- Where they're going;
- Where they're exhibiting;
- Where they're speaking;
- What they're reading; and
- Where they've been published.

A quick click through to those events/publications/companies will provide you with a wealth of valuable and immediately useable intelligence.

The final word:
What gets measured gets done

Throughout the book we have looked at why visibility has to be your watchword when it comes to business development. We've looked at the different ways to achieve visibility, the groups you need to be visible to, and the various core activities that are best suited to the different personalities that inhabit the legal profession.

You will now have ideas as to how you can generate greater visibility to the right people, in the right areas. So, now I'm going to share with you the secret that can turn all of those ideas into work. That secret is *action*.

While you can never guarantee an individual marketing initiative will generate a return, I will guarantee with absolute certainty that if you don't do anything, you *will not* generate a return! Once you come up with a plan (or even an intention), you need to put it into action.

However, as we've already discussed, you have a day job – fee earning – and therefore you only have a finite amount of time to dedicate to marketing and business development. This means you have to measure what you do, set yourself deadlines, and monitor progress.

How to set objectives
The best objectives are SMART and that means:

Specific
Don't choose anything woolly or meaningless like 'build profile' or 'create brand awareness'; be specific. Specifically, say:

- What job titles you want to meet in what industries;

- Which professions you want to build up relationships with (and name the organisations and members of those organisations you think would benefit you most);
- Which conferences you want to attend;
- Which events you want to speak at;
- Which networking groups you need to join; and
- Which titles you want to be published in.

Measurable

Put numbers next to them:

- How many new targets do you want to start conversations with?
- How many new professionals do you want to build relationships with?
- How many conferences do you want to attend?
- How many speaking slots do you want?
- How many times will you attend your chosen networking groups? How many new business cards will you collect each time you go?
- How many editorials do you want to write/publish during the year?

When it comes to measurement and to charting your progress, this is the key step. Having those numbers will allow you to tick off successes and reenergise and re-enthuse yourself during the predictable fallow periods that will be forced on you by work pressures at different points during the year.

Achievable

You are not going to have two coffee meetings with clients per day or write and deliver two presentations per month. Make sure your numbers are achievable. As a rough guide, I'd suggest you should be looking at something like:

- One new conversation with one new target per month;
- One new conversation with one new professional a month;
- Attend three (major) conferences per year;
- Write and deliver four presentations (internal and/or external) per year;
- Attend two networking meetings per month; and
- Have four editorials published in different titles during the year.

Moreover, keeping things achievable is a massive psychological boost. Constantly falling short of your targets is hugely demotivating, but crossing off your goals is always going to give you a boost, irrespective of what stage of your career you are at. It also shows others in your team, department, or practice area that it can be done, which – given the part internal competition tends to play within the professional services – is a powerful motivator for those around you.

Relevant
If you are a private client lawyer, there is little point in attending the Chartered Institute of Personal Development's local meeting. If you are an IP/IT lawyer, there is little point in being published in *The Charity Times*. Coming back to the point about time constraints (not to mention budgetary constraints), you need to be selective, so concentrate on the initiatives and vehicles that are most likely to deliver a return for your particular practice area.

I am certainly not discounting the theory of 'you never know who knows who' (i.e. anyone you speak to could know someone who needs your help). This is a proven and productive method of generating enquiries. I am, however, strongly advocating that when it comes to setting objectives you concentrate on the theory of 'the most likely' so that the odds of your efforts succeeding are as stacked in your favour as they can be.

Timed

Setting a deadline is a great way of adding a bit of focus and putting a bit of (gentle) pressure on yourself. You will have noticed in the examples in the 'Achievable' section above that I have used very specific frequencies. If you employ similar time-frames you will know immediately if you are:

- On course;
- A little behind; or even
- Ahead.

In that way, you can take any necessary actions that may be required to get things back on track. You can also see if your targets are too low. If you are hitting your targets with ease, they are too soft so you may want to increase them slightly as you get into the groove of your business development plan.

Measuring yourself

Back in Chapter 5, we looked at a simple one-page grid you could use to monitor your referrer management. This can be easily adapted and appropriated to measure your general coffee (or tea, beer, prosecco, or organic smoothie) contact plan.

In this more general context, the grid we use is the one illus-trated in Figure 1. Not only is this a simple, time-efficient tool (it takes seconds to update it as all you need to do is drop an X in the right square), it also makes sure you are seeing the people you should see, and as often as you should be, by reminding you the meeting you committed to when you completed the grid is coming up and an invite needs to be sent.

	Jan	Feb	Mar	Apr	May	Jun	Jul	Aug	Sep	Oct	Nov	Dec
Contact 1												
Contact 2												
Contact 3												
Contact 4												
Client 1												
Client 2												
Client 3												
Referrer 1												
Referrer 2												
Referrer 4												
Industry Body												

Figure 1: Coffee contact plan.[1]

When we introduce this into our client work, the reaction isn't only that this is a quick and easy way to manage personal contact but that the thought process around deciding who should be on your list is also hugely valuable. After all, when was the last time you sat down and actively identified the 10 or 12 most productive sources of work for your practice?

Multiple measuring (and motivating)

Once you have chosen your activities and the volume and frequency at which you will do them (and of course the easiest way to measure progress), you can roll reporting into your team and/or departmental meetings. Let me say from the off that this is definitely not meant to be a name-and-shame exercise (although there is the added benefit that a feeling of competition will spur serial non-doers into action!). It is meant instead to be a sharing exercise where you can report your successes and your progress alongside everyone else.

It is also a chance to discuss why things have or have not worked, which is invaluable in terms of refining your plans and choice of activities to ensure your marketing is always as time- and cost-efficient as it can be, as well as an opportunity for some informal training and personal development.

And again, we are not talking about a cascade of marketing activity. If everyone around the table came in having achieved two things during the preceding month – two things that are relevant to your practice area and that ensure you are ticking the networking, writing, speaking, and research boxes – how much further ahead would you be? How much more visibility would you be creating in your chosen markets?

Exactly!

References

1. Again, if you would like a fully working excel sheet housing this tool, you can drop me an email at douglas@tenandahalf.co.uk and I'll gladly send it over.